Starting Your Super Successful Face Painting Business

Sherrill Church
Mimicks Face Painting

Starting Your
Super Successful
Face Painting Business

ISBN   978 0 9576265 0 8

First Edition 2013 Great Britain

Copyright ©2013 Sherrill Church

Published by Mimicks

DEDICATION

This book is dedicated simply to
everyone who ever told me that
face painting isn't real work and that
I should get a proper job!

CONTENTS

Chapter 9 - Putting Systems in Place

Chapter 10 - Legal Requirements

Chapter 11 - Hygiene Techniques and Procedures

Sample Documents

Resources

ACKNOWLEDGMENTS

Mimicks Face Painting has been on a long journey over the past two decades and without the commitment and dedication of employed staff it wouldn't have been possible. So I'd like to thank:

Jo, Cathy, Nicole, Anna, Katie, Rachel, Natalie, Clare, Lucy, Emma, Kellie, Rachel, Carol, Emma, Beckie, Aimee, Sue, Natalie, Louise, Erica, Lian, Beckie, Hayley, Sarah, Amy, Reema, Vicky, Gemma, Vanessa, Kayleigh, Charlotte, Ashmi, Sam, Tara, Jayne, Kerrie, Marie, Rachel, Megan, Victoria, Sam, Leanne, Emily, Louise, Emma, Chloe, Vicki, Ruth, Becca, Emma, Anna, Tania, Kelly, Hayley, Avaneet, Stephanie, Phillipa, Helen, Keri, Kayleigh

....and the biggest acknowledgement and thanks go to
Roger my husband, Ashlea my daughter and Brenda my mum

Oh and of course my much loved son who spent many a weekend on his own fending for himself because his mother was in a field in a different part of the country somewhere. Thank you Asa for looking after the cat!

INTRODUCTION

Have you ever heard the expression "You'll never make money out of face painting". You probably have, many times.

Think back to those times and of the people that made this statement to you. Were they friends and family, urging you to take on a 'proper' job, thinking that face painting was just a fad. Or were they acquaintances that perceived you as some mad struggling artist, not wanting to put into the Monday to Friday 9 to 5 routine, or maybe they were face painters themselves who had dabbled a bit here and there but who never gave it complete commitment so therefore never made very much money.

Those people are out there, and yes they will try to knock you back and persuade you otherwise, but please take it from me as a person who has literally been there, done that, bought the t-shirt and now written the book: "You can make a very good income running a face painting business and all it takes is a desire to do so, a full-blown passion for the industry and a big commitment to do what it takes to become successful. Easy!

People will often ask me "How have you made your face painting company so successful" and "How did you get started in all of this".

Well it happened a long, long time ago and purely by accident. It was in the summer of 1990 that I came across the idea of face painting and how I could make a business out of it. We were on holiday and I became intrigued by a woman painting children with a product that I'd never seen before. Now my children, Ashlea and Asa, at that time were very young and obviously they were keen to have some sort of master-piece painted on their faces along with the countless other children. They had had their faces painted (or should I say crayoned) many times before, but not like this, oh no this was very different, a complete work of art.

So Ashlea was painted beautifully as a Snow Queen and spent all day not licking her lips for the fear of her stunning blue lip colour being washed away, and Asa opted for the Ninja Turtle (typical boy thing then)! Wow they looked fantastic.

I spent the complete holiday mapping out a business idea in my head which just grew and grew over those seven days. I couldn't wait to get home to start the process of my new company. However, one slight problem. How was I going to find out about this remarkable new paint thingy that the face painter was using. I couldn't just go up to her and ask her, as she probably wanted to keep it her little secret. Also I had made it a bit obvious that I was checking her out as I spent a lot of time peering over her shoulder and then rushing off to the cloakroom to draw out the masterpieces she was creating onto a scrappy piece of paper. She must have known I was up to something and was possibly going to pinch her ideas.

Eventually I plucked up the courage to go and ask her about this product she was using. This is how it went:
"Err hello. I was just wondering about the paint that you're using. I work in a nursery school (big fib) and we do face painting on the kids but just use those crayon things. The paint you're using looks really good. What is it"?

Well she didn't really look too pleased about my upfront question. This was her baby. Why should she give trade secrets away to just anyone. I continued to babble on about this nursery school that I supposedly worked in and that the paint would be so much better for the children.

It worked. Reluctantly she reached into her kit box (with a sigh) and rummaged around for a lid from a paint pot, and handed it over to me. Great stuff. That one little Grimas face paint lid gave me a fantastic business opportunity.

Now I could have continued my conversation with her to try to find out where to actually buy this product. But the look on her face said that was all she was willing to give way, and don't even dare to try to find out anything else. I thanked her and walked away with a huge smile and a golden opportunity clutched firmly in my fist.

And that was how it started.

On arriving home I immediately set to work on my new project. I put in the hours around the business I was already running, and of course my usual household chores and tending to the children as a single parent.

The first big problem I needed to overcome was where I buy this Grimas face paint from. I searched for days. It wasn't easy to source a product then as in those days the Internet wasn't around. I went to libraries, I searched the Yellow Pages, and I visited craft shops, stationery shops, beauty salons and make-up counters but still couldn't find this paint anywhere. I made countless telephone calls to anyone and everyone. I wasn't going to let the mere problem that I couldn't find this stuff beat me. Oh no, I was on a mission and I would succeed.

I finally had my eureka moment when I walked into my local fancy dress shop, and to my pure amazement and delight they sold it. A very small selection of Grimas Face Paints, stored in a box under the counter. I bought the lot, along with some brushes and sponges. Looking back I think that business investment and start-up package was about £46 in total. Not a lot really when you think of the profit in the years to come that I would make.

So back at home I set to work on my kids trying out this wonderful product and the fantastic effects and designs that you could achieve. I have a creative and artistic flair naturally and found that I took to it with ease. Using the scrappy drawings that I had scribbled down whilst on holiday I was able to produce snow queens and ninjas, tigers and pussy-cats, butterflies and parrots and amazing beech and sunset scenes.

Ah that's easy I hear you say. And yes you are so right, but back then the normal crayon type face paintings had been either a clown or a rag doll – and not really much else. So you see these faces were a complete artistic transformation and very rarely seen.

The local carnival and fun-fair was due in town on the following Saturday and I thought that this would be a great place to start to show off my new found talent. I had three days to prepare and practise for it and I pulled all stops out.

I drew some face painting designs out on paper and placed them in a folder and proudly labelled it 'Face Painting Designs'. A friend made me a sturdy collapsible table that I could sit the children on. I got cracking on my sewing machine and made a tablecloth. And I purchased a few other items that I felt would be needed for my new enterprise.

The Saturday morning arrived and I packed all my goodies into a plastic bag (how unprofessional was that, I could have bought a kit box) and set off to the recreation ground where the funfair was, with my kids in tow. I screwed the nuts and bolts into my table and positioned all my products out nice and orderly; I painted Ashlea and Asa as a promotional advertisement and waited for my first customer. That afternoon I painted 11 happy little children and stunned their parents with my work of art. I was well pleased and my confidence soared.

Then disaster struck. A council officer came up to me to ask to see my 'pedlar's license' as I was on council ground and needed a permit. Oh no, what was a 'pedlars license'. Where would I get one of them from? Help. She said I had to pack away immediately as I was breaking the law. I started to place my products back into the plastic bag when out of the blue the fairground owner came waltzing up demanding to know what was going on. The councillor told him that I was being move on as I had no permit. The funfair guy replied "She doesn't need a permit, she's with us, and she's part of the fun-fair". The councillor looked at me and said "Is that right, are you with the fairground?" Well I wasn't going to say no was I?

The fairground guy picked up my table and moved me about 6 feet over so I was actually on his grassed area. The councillor shook her head in disbelief and off she went. I couldn't thank Mr. Stevens, the funfair owner, enough. He had helped me out in a very awkward situation which I knew nothing about way back then.

That Saturday evening came and along came the carnival procession and along came the crowds. My face painting set-up was right amongst all of the children's rides and I became absolutely bombed out. I worked continuously for 3 hours with a lengthy queue and only giving up when the light had faded. What an evening. I had earned £150 in such a short space of time and had provided some entertainment value to the people watching and had painted 60 very happy children.

And so within two weeks I had set up a new business and had found a lucrative move into a very new market. From that first Saturday to well over two decades later I have never looked back.

Check out the Mimicks Face Painting website at
www.mimicks.co.uk

And that's how I did it and how I started *my* super
successful face painting business ....and now it's time for you to
Start *Your Very Own* Face Painting Business

CHAPTER 1

Starting Out

A Step in the Right Direction

Congratulations . . . . you've decided to become a part of this fun, crazy, hectic and lucrative world that many thousands of like-minded individuals have come to know and love with a strong undeniable passion. From the very first moment that you find yourself thrown into the realms of providing your face painting service at birthday parties, fetes and fun-days and company run events you'll never look back as you become bitten by the bug. The face painting bug! Your hunger for anything face painting will significantly increase and you'll find that all of your spare time will be put into watching video tutorials on how to improve your techniques, you'll be scanning the countless websites that entice you in with an array of tempting products and equipment to purchase and you'll be participating on the forums as you'll have countless questions that need to be answered.

And on that note I'd like to say 'Welcome to our face painting community – you're heading on a fantastic journey'.

You've no doubt seen the fun and creative side of the industry as you've peered over the shoulder of a face painter, along with the huge earning potential and have probably thought to yourself 'I could do that'. That's usually how it all begins. However, for some the very thought of starting up, where to go for advice, what products to use and how to find out about all the different types of events that you can attend can be a little over-whelming for a new business owner. Well at long last this book your holding in your hands will have all those important questions answered, and more so, as you dive head-long in to your distinctly successful face painting business.

If this is your very first step into running a business you may feel a little unsure of your capabilities. You may be concerned about how to effectively run a business with regards to company protocol, legal administration and documenting records, action planning and just basically getting the word out there now that you are a business owner. Scary stuff maybe? Well not so. Often I hear people say that they can't run a business, they wouldn't have a clue what to do, and they have no family or friends already running an enterprise to advise them, and so on and so on with all the excuses under the sun. It's wise to remember here that running a business is actually very easy to do, very easy – it's often the case of the people running the business that make it difficult. Business doesn't need to be difficult. These people put obstacles in their own way, these people put up objections to their own success and they just don't discipline themselves when it comes down to taking consistent action in things that matter in order to make their business grow. They become stagnated and complacent with no real desire to achieve what they really can if they put their minds to it. Now I'm not saying that it's going to be an easy ride as you will need to put in a lot of time and effort and you'll have failures and successes along the way, and if this is your very first business venture you will get a great sense of self-satisfaction as you see your baby grow, no matter what route you wish to follow with regards to how many events you anticipate doing on a yearly basis.

At this moment in time you may be unsure of the route that your face painting venture will take. Are you simply looking to provide just a handful of community based events over the year and maybe a couple of children's birthday parties each month, or are you looking to eventually quit your day job and run your face painting service as your main source of yearly income? Either way there are countless opportunities out there for you to proceed in the direction that you so wish and with the video tutorials, the vast product ranges, the chat rooms and now this book on how to start your face painting business productively will most certainly put you on the right path to reach your desired destiny, no matter how small or how large your aspirations are.

This is such a great industry to be a part of. Its fun, very rewarding, satisfying and it can eventually earn you a level of income you'd be quite surprised at. However it does occasionally have its downsides as with the very nature of our service industry people don't take it, or us, seriously. They look at what we do as 'just a little bit of face painting'. You will have plenty of nay-sayers that will knock you back by saying that it's not a proper job, or they'll ask what your real job is, or they'll say you can't make money with face painting or they'll say it's a five-minute wonder. Negative influences from those around you will be a huge barrier to your achievement; however you want to measure that. I've heard all those pessimistic comments before and regardless of them (or in spite) I've been in this five-minute wonder for well over two decades now with my daughter Ashlea following in my footsteps. If I wasn't earning serious money and making a healthy living from my business don't you think I would have quit by now, as would many of the other hundreds and hundreds of highly successful world-wide face painters running very profitable ventures.

Family and friends might even warn you that being self-employed is risky compared to having the comfort zone of employment. Well quite the reverse actually. Being employed you have no choice in the matter whether your job is 'safe' or not. Recently we have seen jobs in the public and private sector being taken away from hard-working, long-standing employees, who then weave their way to the job centres looking for new hope. These individuals have had their lifestyle pulled away from them without as much as a blink of an eyelid.

So being in business for yourself is far less risky as you are the master of your destiny, the creator of your Universe; you make the choices and the changes to suit your needs and your customer needs based on the economy. So no, being self-employed is far less risky than being employed as you are the decision maker on how successful you want your business to be.

To succeed at the highest level in our face painting industry you will need a passionate reason to do so, remembering that what you achieve comes purely from what you believe in and what actions you decide to put in place to see your business grow. And whether you've just started out as a completely new face painter or have already dabbled a bit here and there or are now a seasoned professional in the industry with many years under your belt, discovering how to reach your destiny is absolutely crucial to *your* business success.

Why Are You in Business?

Have you sat down and really thought about why you want to have your own business. Is it because you don't want to be 'employed' by someone else anymore? Is it so that you can be in charge of your own vocation? Is it the status that could be attached to running your own show? Is it because you think you will be in a better financial situation or is it because you want to be able to pick the hours you work to suit you and your needs and your family needs?

There are so many objectives (reasons why) that you need to put in place before starting out, you need to search deep and really decide on what the main purpose is for you to enter into your own business venture. You will of course through your soul-searching come up with reasons that you may feel you will not be suited to being solely self-employed, and maybe need the continued added security of being a part-time or full-time employee as well, which is a good idea in the beginning as a new business needs time to develop and evolve in its early stages.

It will be a helpful exercise to consider the following aspects and put them into priority order as your main reasons for being a small business owner along with listing any influencing negative beliefs that you may have:

- Money – how much do you want to earn, how much do you need to earn to just scrape by, how much do you need to earn to be comfortably off and how much do you need to earn to be completely financially independent?

- Type of Work – how much of the work involved are you happy to do by yourself? Does this include all the face painting service provision, the administration on running a business, the paperwork, the book-keeping and the very important marketing? How much of the work is satisfying or unsatisfying to you, do you need to update your skills in order to advance in any particular area?

- Working Hours – how much time are you likely to spend actually providing your service, how much time is needed for running the business and pushing it through its stages of growth, are you able to cope with the stresses and the strains of being self-employed?

- Social Hours – how much free time are you looking to have, are you prepared to work seven days a week on your venture and always being 'open for business' having little or no time for social aspects?

- Independence and Achievement – how important is it to you to feel valued in what you do, are you able to make informed decisions quickly by yourself, are you able to set standards within your business that can be met and will you be happy to work in isolation? Are you confident in your business matters knowing that the buck stops with you?

- Family – is your partner, spouse, family and friends behind you 100% in the running of your business, if not then why not, are you and they aware that you may become blinkered towards your business and that it may take control over every other aspect of your life? Face Painting is very addictive and you can quite easily become a 'junkie' to the cause once you get bitten by the bug.

After you have drawn up your list of objectives for why you want to be in business, it will give you a clearer picture of what you are setting out to achieve along this route and it will also prove to be a very good exercise for those already in the throes of business activity.

You will discover over time that being in business for yourself can be more demanding and tougher than you ever imagined. You may worry about the security of your business, the financial flow of customer income and the dependency of the business on you as you may feel that you are irreplaceable and indispensable.

Do you know what will happen to your booked events if you're unable to work due to possible ill-health, maybe through a bad sprain to your hand or even a twisted ankle preventing you from driving, and what about taking a holiday – will there be strategies in place for times like these? Are you committed enough to be the chief cook and bottle washer all rolled into one.

Success Doesn't Happen Overnight

In the first few months of any new business, and sometimes for the first few years, things progress at a slow pace. Don't become too discouraged if you feel you're spending a lot of time and money in getting your business going, building up customer databases, spending out on products and equipment, enrolling on industry led courses and workshops – with little or no return to show for it. This is usual practice. It's wise to remember here that if business was profitable from day one everyone would be doing it and making a fortune.

All highly successful face painters started at the very beginning, and this may very well be the place where you are now. Yes its daunting and scary, yes it's thrilling and exciting – but with a pre-determined desire to achieve success, however you want to measure that success, you will as long as you realise that 'Rome wasn't built in a day'. Take small baby steps, day by day, month by month, and see the outstanding results that you can achieve as your business grows right before your very eyes.

It's very difficult to determine for each person when their business becomes 'full-time' enabling your yearly earnings to be regarded as making a living. Everyone's lifestyle and financial situation is so different. One person may be able to give up their part-time or full-time job on earning just £10,000 from face painting per year and others may need to earn £40,000. You also need to remember that a lot of face painters that have been in the industry for many years also have other areas of income to support their business. They could be a training provider, a product supplier or even offering other allied services such as pamper parties, balloon modelling and even cake decorating. So it's not all about just providing your face painting service that will enable you to give up your day job. In our very seasonal industry you'll need to think outside the paint pot and strive for expansion in other related activities.

By not becoming despondent and giving up at the first hurdle you are moving in the right direction and you will have to put in to get out. Time and money spent will not be wasted as long as you continue to push forward as hard as you can, remain focused on your goals and stay dedicated and passionate towards your business venture.

What Does It Take To Be Your Own Boss?

Decisiveness and Discipline. The Double D's. For sure! In fact everything you do to do with your business and also your personal life have to have the Double D's attached to it. Make everything you do a conscious *decision* and then add a *discipline* to it – in other words you've made a conscious decision to purchase this book and now you'll need to put a discipline in place to read it from start to finish.

You naturally discipline yourself on a daily basis in all areas of your life from getting up in the morning when the alarms goes off to eating breakfast and brushing your teeth. Think of all the other times throughout your day that you do things as a discipline, an unconscious decision, a necessity to function, without even thinking about it. You do many, many things on auto-pilot. Get into the habit of making everything you do within your business life a Double D.

So with that in mind you'll need to *discipline* yourself to market your business effectively in order to get more customers, you'll need to *discipline* yourself to send out booking confirmations and invoices, you'll need to *discipline* yourself to arrive at your events on time, *discipline* yourself to order more face painting kit so that you don't run out, *discipline* yourself to do the daily, weekly and monthly paperwork in order to run your business as a smooth operation. Conscious decisions will need to be made frequently and then you'll need to put disciplines in place to actually see them through.

Discipline will come into every aspect of your working day, including responding to messages that have been left on your phone or answering every email enquiry that comes in, to networking with other like-minded individuals, updating your website or blog or promotional material and always being ready to provide a first-class service that will keep your customers coming back for more.

It's all very well having many wonderful and exciting ideas for your face painting business but until you actually make a decision to act on all those wonderful and exciting ideas and put a discipline in place to see them through, your face painting venture may just as well be only a hobby. Like I've already said, it's you that will be the chief cook and bottle washer and it's you that will be accountable for every last little thing that has to do with running a successful venture. Unfortunately there is no hierarchy, no manager or no colleague to support you and to give you a 'to do' list or to act as a sounding board or to give you a kick up the bum. Yeah sure, there are plenty of people in our industry who are eager to pass on their knowledge to the up and coming newbies in the community regardless as to whether that's through online tutorials, courses, chat-rooms, articles, magazines and the like – but the buck stops there as it's up to you to put their sound advice into practice and discipline yourself to see those business strategies through. Like it or not, you're on your own.

On the brighter side, however, being your own boss is a truly remarkable and exhilarating position to be in. You decide on your daily activities, whether that's servicing your customers, visiting a trade show and networking or doing the book-keeping. You decide what times to work at the weekend and the times during the profitable season. You decide on your earning potential by setting your prices with good profit margins, or to even take part-time employment to run alongside your business to help pay the bills in the short-term. It's your business, so you'll call all the shots on just how successful it will be.

In the next chapter we'll take a look at all the distractions that you'll come across on a daily basis and how to manage them effectively. But for now discipline yourself to really think about why you are in business and what level of success do you actually want to achieve from it.

CHAPTER 2

Working From Home

Dealing With Distractions

Regardless of the fact that your face painting activities will take place on location in other people's homes, or at showground's and at a variety of company establishments, you are still considered to be 'working from home'. It's here that all your business administration will be undertaken. There are many advantages to working from home and for starters the overheads are extremely low, and it's also very convenient having all your business assets in one place.

If you're fortunate enough to have space in your home to convert one small room, say a bedroom into an office, you'll find this a prime benefit. Even when running a small business you'll find that you'll have many files, folders, books, stationery, pencils, pens, rubbers and rulers that need to have their own space for storage that can be easily retrievable on a daily basis.

If you are unable to dedicate an 'office-room' then it is advisable to purchase some kind of bookcase with doors on, so that you can keep all your business paperwork neatly organised and in one place.

Without the luxury of the spare room, maybe you can turn a little corner of your home into 'your personal office space'. Take a look around your home; there must be somewhere where you can place a small desk and bookcase, someplace where you can concentrate on the job in hand to build your business. Aside from the space that you'll be in when you're providing your face painting service you'll also need space to work on your business and this will generally be done at home. You'll find that you will work a lot smarter in a more organised business setting, and your mental attitude towards it will sharpen when there is paperwork to be done as you won't have to gather together all the info you need before you even turn the computer on!

There's nothing worse than looking for a supplier invoice or your rate card and having to rummage through the stack of ironing, the pile of newspapers in the corner of the lounge or through all the lovely pictures that the kids have been drawing whilst sitting at the kitchen table! Your sanity will be calmer if you know where you can lay your hands on vital information in an instant. Also, customers will lose faith in you if you have to go searching for your bookings diary!

As your venture expands and new systems are put in place it's essential that you spend adequate time promoting, developing and improving your business in an environment that is productive for your needs. Your business is relying solely on you to make it a success and the amount of effective time and effort that requires complete concentration is an essential business building principle.

Working from home, however, can mean distractions - and plenty of them. Sometimes it can be hard to get going on your business tasks because stuff keeps getting in the way. Stuff, as we'll call it, can be a major disruption to our business life. Stuff can come in all shapes and sizes and could include family and friends turning up unexpectedly, the dog barking at the postman, the kids needing your attention and the cooking and cleaning chores to be done. You can end up feeling like your banging your head against a brick wall, you can't see the wood for the trees, and instead of your workload reducing, it's escalating.

Your time is your best resource and under no circumstances should you allow anyone to steal it away from you. Most people do not place a value on their time and likewise will not value your time. Interruptions and disruptions in your daily activities will mount up minute by minute and they will eat away and prevent you from meeting your deadlines which inevitably will have to be put off.

We all know how our daily plans can somehow go adrift from what we had initially planned because of stuff happening, and it is generally stuff that needs your attention now as people unexpectedly spring things on you – some good, some bad. The clasp that you had on your time in the morning has, against your will, gone. At the end of each and every day you need to re-focus, re-organize and re-establish your priorities for the following day. This way you will be able to start the next day fresh, with a re-evaluated list.

All This Stuff Is Holding Me Back

Here is a brief list of the 'stuff' that you may encounter as a distraction in your working from home environment:

- The telephone ringing
- Family and friends visiting
- Hesitation and faffing around
- Cooking, cleaning and shopping to be done
- Kids to collect from school
- The dog barking
- The double glazing guy knocking on your door
- The kids shouting and screaming
- The television is way too loud
- Music is blaring out

....and the list could go on and on as each and every one of us has other personal distractions to deal with in our lives.

Let's take each point that's listed above and discuss each one further in order to eliminate them as a distraction:

- The telephone ringing – a distraction yes, but a priority to answer as it could be an enquiry from a customer or a booking to be confirmed. To avoid taking calls from family and friends at an inopportune moment make sure that their numbers are displayed on ringing, and this way you can flick onto answer-machine if necessary.

- Family and friends visiting unexpectedly – you are running a business and there is work to be done so let these people know of your 'no visit' times. You wouldn't dream of turning up at your best friend's office in the middle of the day just for a friendly chit-chat would you? Don't let them do the same to you. Unfortunately people tend to think that those who work from home are just sitting around drinking coffee and watching day-time TV. Let them know that it's not like that at all as you have priorities, schedules and above all a business to build.

- Hesitation – JFDI! (my most favourite saying). Take action in your tasks, duties and key areas that will put money straight into your bank account. Man Yana, Man Yana – always putting off until tomorrow. Stop looking at lists and tweaking them, stop tidying your desk and stop shuffling paperwork. This is all faffing around and isn't pro-active at all. We're all guilty of faffing around at some time or another and believe me, becoming too pernickety about what style and size of font to use in your leaflet isn't worth spending copious amounts of time on!

- Cooking, cleaning and shopping – this stuff can easily be delegated to another person especially if you have older children or a partner who is supportive in your business endeavours. Devise some sort of rota and possibly a reward to go with the chore for the kids.

- Kids to collect from school – join or organise some sort of school run. Seek out the other work from home mums or dads and arrange a thorough system for home-time collection. You could even go as far as each parent takes it in turn for a week to take the kids back to theirs for a couple of hours after school. This way if there are 4 of you that means for 3 weeks out of 4 you will have an extra 30 hours of input time. Yes 30 hours. Think of what you could do with all that extra time!

- The dog barking – can be so annoying but you will find that if you break off for 20 minutes during the day to take the dog out or just to go for a brisk stroll around the block by yourself (without a dog), you'll be able to collect your thoughts and divulge in some very necessary thinking time. You'll find that you will be able to concentrate better on business matters after a little time in the fresh air. It happens to me quite often when I'm out walking Barley and Willow, my Shetland Sheepdogs, as I'm able to hear myself think better.

- The double glazing guy knocking on your door – just don't answer the door, simple as that!

- Kids shouting, television too loud and music from the bedrooms are all just part of family life, so enjoy them. There's no point in getting stressed-out about it because children grow up so fast and are moved out before you know it! Make a decision not to worry too much about this type of distraction and instead enjoy it, and if you can only get 10 minutes business administration input out of each hour when the kids are at home, so be it as family life is very precious and important and will aid to your harmonious work-life balance.

Undertaking business administration from home does have its challenges as our home comforts are all around us and it can be so very easy to be busy, being busy. So to help you through everything that will be essential in your business and daily life you need to make important decisions and set disciplines to see them through (the Double D's again) in the ever-feuding battle between Organisation vs. Disorganisation. And to become smartly organised and on top of your game in your face painting business you need to think about everything, and I mean everything, that your daily and weekly life throws at you and devise a structured time plan to help you through it all in your working from home environment.

Any time that you need help with self-discipline issues, you need to focus and revisit your business purposes that we discussed earlier. Is that to run your own business and to be your own boss, working from home in the hours that suit your lifestyle, being responsible for your own income and your own destiny, doing something that you'll love doing? If all of the above is important, you'll need to prioritise and kick into shape all the distracting stuff that is happening around you. Put the phone on answer-machine and leave the messy kitchen until later on in the day. It's surprising how much you can get done if you just have a clear 3-hour stretch in front of you.

To be effective in your working day you need to work to a specific time plan. You must be strict and impose these deadlines on yourself, because unfortunately no one else will do it for you. You'll also find that working against a deadline is a sure-fast way to kick yourself into action in order to accomplish the task. I know I work extremely well if I have deadlines to meet and my back is up against the wall. I suppose this fear of failing to meet the deadline pushes you to pull all stops out and to work every given hour available. The greatest invention the world has ever known is the deadline. Without it nothing would have gotten done, or been accomplished or ever achieved – a great little quote from an un-known author.

You need to claw back those wasted minutes by not allowing others to peck away at it. A 'Do Not Disturb' sign is not just for hotel rooms. You should make a practice of hanging one on your office door, kitchen door, and front door, to warn the time demons that you are stuck into a project that needs your undivided attention and you will not be available for interruptions until the sign is removed. Try having as many clocks around you as you can, as this will play an important role in your time management. You don't want to be saying, "Where did the time go". You need to know where the time went. Don't lose it and don't let anyone else steal it from under your nose.

You may be thinking to yourself at this stage that surely running a face painting business is easy-peasy, can't be that much to it, and it's generally only done on Saturday's and Sunday's? Well yes it can be like that if you only intend on doing a handful of events here and there, but if you want to earn serious money from your new venture then you will need to put in plenty of administration and marketing time, and by this I mean structured and planned time that you've scheduled in so that you can explore ways on how to develop and grow your business so that you are meeting your objectives on why you want to work for yourself. Time, and more importantly how you manage your time is an important foundation for your business success.

Are You Busy Being Busy?

When you're running a business, regardless as to whether it's an established home-based one or a brand-new start-up you need to be organized with your time you need to think about everything that you need and want to do this week, next week, next month and for the year ahead and put some structure into your planning for the future.

Below is a *fictitious* scenario of the day in the life of someone who is running a home-based business, or rather trying to run a home-based business (it could be any business) but what they're actually doing is – **being busy being busy**. Could this be familiar?

7.00am: Rise, breakfast, get kids ready for school
8.00am: Take kids to school
8.45am: Home from school, have a coffee
9.15am: Washing up, tidy kitchen, vacuum lounge
10.00am: Switch on TV just to catch up with current affairs
10.30am: Put the washing in and then have a coffee

11.00am: Turn on computer and wait to logon to the Web

11.15am: Look at to do list and make another to do list

11.45am: Hang out washing and have another coffee

12.15pm: Go back to the list and choose which task to start

12.20pm: Start task – half heartedly and shuffle paperwork

1.00pm: Lunch time

1.45pm: Back to the computer and check emails

2.15pm: Take dogs for walk or have a brisk stroll

2.50pm: A quick coffee before the school run

3.05pm: Leave home to collect the kids from school

3.30pm: Nip to the shops for potatoes and milk

4.15pm: Home, turn TV on for kids, and sort homework

4.30pm: Sit with kids, watch TV, quality time together

5.30pm: Start cooking the evening meal

6.15pm: Sit down together to eat meal

6.40pm: Wash, wipe up and tidy kitchen

7.15pm: Kids bath-time

7.45pm: Kids story-time

8.00pm: Kids bed-time

8.05pm: Turn on TV to catch up on soaps, have a coffee

9.00pm: Visit computer and go on social media sites

10.30pm: Have a coffee

11.00pm: Bed-time, after a busy day being busy!

Adding up the proactive business minutes above comes to 70, yes 70 minutes, that's just over one hour's worth of work in a whole day. Unfortunately that's not how to grow a business, and if you plan on being successful, super successful in your face painting business then you need to make every minute and every hour count towards progression, financial progression.

Once you get going with your face painting business I challenge you to keep a diary and into it jot down only the minutes and hours that you were actually doing something pro-active to move your business forward. This doesn't include doing your face painting events and such-like, as that is your service provision which is not ultimately responsible for your business growth. The moments to capture are purely those that you did to work on your business rather than in your business. Will you be surprised at your result?

Making Effective Use of Your Time

If you're running a small part-time face painting business AND you're also holding down another job to make ends meet, that can be a double nightmare. A portfolio of employment they call it these days!

Quite often I hear people complaining that they just don't have enough hours in their day, days in their week or weeks in their month to accomplish all they need to do within their business life. It doesn't have to be like that. We all have the same 24 hours and the same 7 days in our week. It's how we utilize all those collective minutes by making each and every one count in order to make them more profitable for our very own businesses.

If you already have a nine to five job during the week and do face painting at the weekends as a side-line your business actions may be very limited to the amount of time you are able to spend on growth. You'll need to take each Saturday and

Sunday as it comes, and if you're not out there face painting you need to be very strict on the disruptions during those hours that you wish to use for business administration and marketing. Ask for help from your partner, if you have one, and get their support where you can. If they too can see the huge future potential that you could have with your face painting company then they will be only too pleased to do whatever it takes to allow you quality time to spend on your business matters, in peace and quiet.

It's all down to organization versus disorganization.

You know you need to put in the hours to run your business effectively, especially if you intend at some stage to give up your other job, but your current commitments elsewhere are such a drain on your time. You may have the additional responsibility of keeping home and bringing up the kids (if you have them) and sometimes it can all get too much. Oh yeah, and then there's your social life – social life, what social life, you must be joking!

You'll need to be 100% committed to your business needs or else you will always battle against time. Not enough time to do the things you want and need to do in order to push your business forward. There are never enough hours in the day, or so it may seem to you. Don't fall into that trap of being busy, being busy and stating that you haven't got enough time . . . you probably have but you just need to make better use of it!

CHAPTER 3

Building Your Brand

What's In a Name?

So we've talked about what it takes with regards to being your own boss and keeping a strict discipline on your time in order to work the business, and probably the next thing on your mind is what to call your new face painting venture. Funnily enough, choosing your business name is usually one of the first things that you'll do. You'll decide to start a face painting business and hey-presto your next immediate thought will be 'What shall I call it'. Before you know it you've started popping all sorts of business names around in your head. This is a usually activity – start business, so immediately decide on the name to call it.

I can remember the day in 1990 when I brainstormed with my Mum on a business name for my fresh new face painting business and I hadn't even painted my very first face yet. I must admit it only took half an hour to come up with the name Mimicks (with one middle M and not two) and it stuck. I didn't think for the life of me that I'd still be running the same business over two decades later. I'm very happy that I got it right all those years ago.

When I named my fairytale party venue, Once Upon A Party, I did do a lot of soul-searching, internet research and planning on that one. I spent months trawling the internet for variations on what was already out there with regards to the combination of a children's party venue with specialised entertainment and when I finally put the combination of the beginning of a fairytale story and the experience of an event I felt I had it just right.

Hopefully you're going to be in business for a long, long time and so choosing a business name is of great importance and not to be taken lightly. Don't always go with your first thought, ponder a little and bounce ideas off family members and friends. The name you choose today should be good enough to be with you next year, in 5 years and in 10 years time. Using a logo to enhance your company name can gain you greater customer awareness and can be used in specific colours and font that will become consistent to your identity and in your branding.

Your business name needs to be easy to pronounce and simple to remember. You'll need as many recommendations as possible in the early stages and you don't want people to avoid this if they have problems in stating clearly who you are or even spelling it out for other people! This also needs to be considered for domain names used in websites – if you choose a business name that has a quirky spelling then you'll find that customers may be unable to find you because they're typing your business name into the search box in the wrong way. An easy mistake for the customer to make don't you think!

The same thing applies with your email address as you need to be 100% happy with it knowing that your customers will not have any difficulty using it and typing it, so don't choose a hard to write one or a hard to spell one or a hard to say one. If you spell things in an unusual manner they are very likely to get miss-spelt as people who are emailing you can make mistakes. Numbered and shortened words come to mind here, such as facepaints4u or facepaintsforyou or facepaintsforu. Which one do you think could be written down incorrectly by the customer? Spelling things in an unusual and peculiar manner just to be cool could result in fewer email queries and domain searches getting through. Try to avoid using your first name too as this will give the impression that you don't have much imagination and have settled for the easy 'my name' option. We're creative people, so our business name should be just as creative. Birth years in email addresses also look very unprofessional, such as yourname1975@yahoo.co.uk, this can indicate your age and the same thing applies for a numbers in email addresses like balloonman4@yahoo.co.uk indicating that he's probably the 4th best.

If you haven't got a domain name and website running for your business using a hotmail account may be your only option, however it doesn't exactly represent a business image along with business branding does it?. Once you have a domain you'll be able to have an array of email aliases with your business name included. Our domain name is mimicks.co.uk and our main email address is info@mimicks.co.uk, plus we also have other prefixes such as sales@..., sherrill@..., ashlea@.... These way enquiries are directed to the relevant inbox. That's so much more professional than sherrill@btinternet.com don't you think?

Is Your Business Name Selling Your Story?

The best type of business name, I'm talking about any business here and not just face painting, should communicate what the business does. Take a look through the Yellow Pages and notice how many of them don't instantly tell you what the business does or offers. Try to think of an angle that you can use to speak volumes with your name which will add value to what you do.

You may have some unique element about you or your service that you can encapsulate in your business name. It should create a 'good-feeling' to your customers, give a clue to your image, and be as original as possible to any other business name regardless of the industry. I often ponder over everyday sayings and then in my head I try to match them up to a business category, any business category. It's such a fun thing to do, probably silly but you should have a go at it. An example of this is the business that sells bathroom design called 'Just Add Water'. What a great business name! A friend of ours is a builder and his company is called 'Brickin' It'! That one's not easily forgotten either.

Before deciding on your choice of business name you should research through the Internet to check if the name is available and hasn't been used elsewhere, preferably on a Global scale. Check out Companies House for registered business names and the Information Commissioners Office for names that are trademarked.

One of my biggest bug-bears (rightly or wrongly as you can decide on this for yourself) is when I see people promoting themselves as 'Professional' or 'Specialist'. Professional Face Painter –really!!! Does it need to be clarified for some reason or another? We're face painters regardless as to whether it's non-profit making or a full-time enterprise. You don't see 'Professional Hair Dresser' or Professional Dentist' or Professional Solicitor'. We all provide a service to our customer or client and we certainly don't need to clarify our status by calling ourselves professional or specialist (sorry but I needed to get that off my chest as it does frustrate me!).

Your business name ideally should be displayed prominently as a notice at all your events as this must include a full postal address and telephone contact information, and on all business stationery such as letterheads, business cards, invoices and receipts. Should you wish to register your name as a Trade Mark then this is easily done and it's not too expensive to do, and it will safeguard you against any other person or business using your name. Trade Marks can be registered on a National or International basis, and this will allow you to use the appropriate symbol against your company name.

Your Unique Selling Proposition

What is going to make you as a face painter stand out from the rest? Why are you so different? What's so unique about you? Your unique selling proposition, that's what. You may have heard other successful business owners talking about their USP.

A unique selling proposition (or unique selling point) can be anything from one word to a sentence or paragraph that you can use in your marketing that completely summarises what you and your business stands for. All the big boys use one, and they can also be referred to as tag-lines or strap-lines. Think about the most popular ones that have become household sayings over the years, such as:

> 'Probably the best in the world' - A well know lager
> 'Lovin It' - A burger
> 'Simples' - A price comparison website
> 'Holidays are coming' - A fizzy drink
> 'Because you're worth it' - A product range

Longer USP's with more substance outlining a promise made to the customer go along the lines of: 'Fresh hot pizza delivered in 30 minutes or less, guaranteed'. The above USP has three messages rolled into one; what's being sold, how quickly you can get it, and a guarantee to confirm that if it's not hot or delivered within 30 minutes or under, you are likely to get it for free! That USP made Tom Monaghan from Dominoes Pizza a multimillionaire and helped to dominate control in the pizza industry, not only in the USA but also the

World, from his first small single outlet. His USP not only incorporates the benefits of a fast delivery service but it also has the added benefit of a guarantee!

Unique selling propositions like that are classics and will stand the test of time and there's no reason at all that you too can't come up with an amazing strap-line to summarize your business benefits.

Your USP can be based on any element of your business – the service, the product, your company policy, business name or even location – anything that you desire, but it's most important mission is to relay the benefits of what you are about or what you can do for your customer. Come up with an influential claim that is yours and only yours on the basis of what you do. A good USP can take months, even years, to come up with so it's not something that needs to be rushed and set in stone with your first thoughts on the matter. Take time to ponder what other businesses have used and try to uncover why they have used it. Think about the services and products that you use on a regular basis and ask yourself 'Does my loyalty to that company have anything to do with their USP, is it delivering an emotion or benefit that is close to my heart'. Become USP receptive and ask questions to yourself about every business, product and service that you happen upon on a daily basis in order to bring to light your very own selling proposition.

CHAPTER 4

Putting Yourself
Out There

your Gateway to Marketing

So your face painting business is all set up and raring to go, or maybe you have been at it for some time now, and one of your biggest worries is how to get more customers – a usual dilemma! If you just sit around waiting for the next event booking to come your way you might have to wait some time unless you become proactive and get amongst it.

If you're new to business and need to build up your customer list, the best place to start is with your family, friends and neighbours. Let's look at each of those on an individual basis.

Family – No doubt you used family members as you went through your practice process, as this is quite usual.

The family members that you have been practicing on now need to be aware that you're building a business that has little or no reputation and that if they want to see you succeed they should be willing to write good-standing testimonials for you about your face painting service. You will be able to use these testimonials to promote yourself. Family members can also be involved in helping to distribute your promotional material to *their* friends that are unknown to you. A good reputation will spread like wild-fire and at this point in time your family will be able to help spread the word to others for you.

Friends – The same approach as above will apply for friends now that you're up and running as a business owner. Certain systems will need to be put in place as this is how you will be earning some income, whether on a part-time basis in the beginning or as a single source of income later on.

You will need to make a decision here about your pricing strategy as a lot of friends will probably be eager to use your face painting service but will they expect something for nothing! To help, you could just ask for a donation of payment against the product that you use or as a gesture for the time spent. You may also be able to do 'tit-for-tat' meaning that they may have a service or something to offer you in exchange for your expertise. Don't fall into the trap here of letting the majority of your friends persuade you to do their little one's party for free, you have to draw the line somewhere. After all you're running a business aren't you and friends and acquaintances should respect this.

In the same instance you will be able to build on your testimonials here and ask each friend for referrals from their family members and any unknown friends and work colleagues that they may have.

Neighbours With Children (direct) – These are people that you see on a regular basis as they are the ones that live in your street.

Make a scheduled time whereby you can go along to their home to put them in the picture about your new business venture. Give them as much information as possible on the face painting service that you provide that you feel would be of interest to them, and leave them with one of your brochures/leaflets. Let them know that you offer a reward system and that they will get a 'special gift' if they refer you to one of their friends or family members who makes a booking with you, and this will be an incentive for them to promote you to whoever they can. There's a lot more about this type of marketing in my other book 'Growing Your Face Painting Business'.

Neighbours (indirect) – These are the people that live in your immediate surroundings, perhaps taking in a handful of roads close by.

Now I'm a great believer that home delivered mail-shots are an absolute waste of time as you can never be sure if you are targeting your market or not because you are unaware of the occupants and their lifestyle that live there. But in the case of promoting your new business venture and the fact that you are also a resident of the immediate area will be well worth the shoe-leather, and you could even go so far as offering them a complimentary discount for being a neighbour of yours.

Building Your First Customer List

To get your customer list built, you need to think of the many other people that you know who your acquaintances are. These people are everywhere and can include your work colleagues (former or current), your spouse's work colleagues, the people who run the corner shop, your dentist or doctor, the guys at the vets, the swimming pool and the gym. Your target list should also include the mums and dads at the school gates and parents at your child's activity clubs.

Take an hour or so to sit down and brainstorm a list of everybody, yes everybody that you know regardless of whether it's just those that you encounter on a daily basis or those that you just see once in a while. You'll be quite surprised at how long your list will be – and any number of these people could have great potential to become one of your customers in the future!

After your list is compiled, your next step will be to organise some sort of time-plan for seeking those people out. For instance one day you could pick the children up from school and hand out leaflets to all the parents there that you know, then head off to the grocery shop to buy some bits and hand out a leaflet or two there, then before going home you have a scheduled appointment to visit the vet with your pet where you can hand out some leaflets there too. That one hour of usual activity could lead to handing out maybe 30 or so leaflets. Put this process into effect with everyone on your list so that you make a point of actually 'bumping' into them because you know where they will be at a certain time of day – and voilà with leaflet in hand – another potential customer has been targeted. Never leave home without a handful of leaflets or business cards ..... just in case!

Joining your local networking group is also a great way to get to know people in your area. If it's a business networking group this will provide you with an opportunity to interact with like minded business owners that will be able to assist you and give you support.

So there's a couple of ways to build your customer list from the very beginning, and with this process of targeting those known to you, you will gradually see the momentum build, which can in fact happen quite quickly.

Organising Your Customer Database

Maybe you already have valuable customer information such as addresses, phone numbers and email addresses stored away somewhere. Well now's the time to start building a database so that information is easily retrievable as and when you need it. You can feed this information into spreadsheets, mail-merges, Word document table formats or even hand-written record cards. By keeping an organised system going right from the very beginning will give you the necessary tools to be able to contact your customers at a moment's notice without having to traipse through diaries, booking forms and sales invoices.

If you're really keen to grow your business to a higher degree and would like to know more about how you can market your business effectively through various forms of advertising and promotion both online and offline, then my book **'Growing Your Highly Profitable Face Painting Business'** is strongly recommended. You can get a copy from Amazon or from our website at www.FacePaintingForProfit.co.uk

CHAPTER 5

Face Painting
At Events

Face Painting Occasions

Face Painters attend a diverse range of events throughout the year, which can include children's birthday parties, school fetes, village fun days, corporate promotions and shows and festivals. The spring and summer months are always the busiest.

After your initial influx of providing face painting at family and friends birthday parties you will then be turning your mind to how you can actually start to make good money and a regular income from your face painting venture. There are an abundance of opportunities for you to choose from and the types of events face painters can be found at are:

Parties – These are private events that the customer books for themselves and they can range from anything to birthday parties, wedding receptions, christening and naming ceremonies to any sort of anniversary party or large family gathering. Fancy dress, Halloween and

Christmas parties are also popular for the private booker. You will find that the majority of your parties will be booked through recommendations, handing out leaflets at other parties and events, putting promotional stickers on painted children with your company details and of course through any online presence such as your website or other social media you may be using.

The age ranges for children's birthday parties varies immensely and you can find yourself being booked for toddler party's right the way through the age ranges to teenage events.

If you have an age policy or restriction in place (more on this later) this will need to be taken into account for a customer booking you for a 1-year old party. Chances are though at this type of event it is usual that older siblings are invited and this will help you to make up the numbers. If however the customer informs you that all the little guests will be 1-year olds then you should let her know that it is very unlikely that all the children at the party will want to be painted for a variety of reasons – or that you just don't do that age group.

This is where setting your prices is very important so that the customer pays for a *group* of children; say up to 10, 15 or 20 will help with your pricing strategy. Let the customer know at the time of booking that she will pay for ten children to be painted as a minimum even if you only paint two on the day. If you set an impractical price to reflect a charge per face painted at the party, then this will mean that if you only paint two children you may very well only earn £6. That's not being business minded at all! The same thing applies here for customers telling you that there will only be 15 children at the party and when you get there you find there are actually 25, or after you've painted the 15 then a further 8 or so Mums and Dads decide at the last minute that they want to be painted too. Have a pricing strategy set that covers a price for group numbers.

Devise some sort of rising price-scale which is dependent on how many children/adults will need to be painted. We start off with a price for 10 guests, and then add £5 for another 5 guests and so on and so on. Our price-scale is pre-set up to 45 guests. The next thing you need to do is to work out your travel-area on say a 15 mile radius and have 3 area-bands (area A, area B and area C). Anyone booking your face painting service that lives in your vicinity of a 15 mile radius pays your lowest prices. Anyone living further than 15 miles away but less than 30 miles away pays your set prices for area B. And those living over 30 miles away pays the set price for area C. This can be easily formatted into a table document which you can print out and keep by your phone for when enquiries are made. It can be very off-putting to a customer if you are unable to give her a price then and there, by saying you'll have to get back to her after you've worked it out. Be on the ball as soon as a prospective customer telephones you – find out how many children and adults would need painting, what area is the party venue in and you'll be able to look on your chart and give her an immediate price.

Eventually as you do more and more parties and other events your application in face painting will speed up and you will find that you will be able to do more faces per hour as time goes on. In the beginning you may only be able to paint 8-10 faces per hour and as your experience grows so will your speed and you may even find yourself painting up to 16 in an hour. With that in mind you need to make sure that the customer is not booking you for 40 faces over a two-hour time scale as you may not be able to complete that request unless you specifically offered only cheek-art. You can easily gauge your speed and the progression of your speed by consciously timing yourself at every event so that you know how many faces you can actually paint in an hour and you'll be able to advise your customer accordingly.

Time-scales are a very important aspect to take into consideration and for a party of 10 children you could inform your customer that this will take you an hour to complete. If you don't let your customer know how long you'll be there for she might be expecting you to stay for the full 2-3 hour party, which could have a massive impact on your prices and any other bookings during the day. So let her know at the time of booking that it's a paint and go system whereby after all those wishing to be painted have been done so you will leave – and not hang around just in case.

How much you charge for a party for the private booker can be dependent on many things. Your skill, the length of time in the industry, how far you'll travel and of course your overheads which will include fuel, insurance, products, etc. You should check out the prices of the competition in your area and set your price to reflect theirs, but on a slightly lower scale as a newcomer to the industry. Never under-cut them by an extensive margin though because all you will do is de-value the industry and you'll be setting yourself up for being cheap which is then very hard to put your prices up. Being in competition with another face painter in your area is just that – its competition. Competition means having fair and similar price indications, similar services, and similar skill. After all, as people continually want to remind you 'It's just a bit of face painting and anyone can do that'. If only they knew!!! Set your prices to reflect the quality of the experience that it will bring to the event. You're basically there to entertain the children so that Mum and Dad can have a little bit of calm to the party for awhile. While you're checking out the prices of other face painters in your area, go one step further and check out the prices of clowns, magicians and Punch and Judy – and you'll soon see what I mean as their prices are usually higher than face painting service charges. Keep your prices keen right from the beginning, be confident right from the beginning and be professional right from the beginning. If you get the awkward question from your customer asking you how long you've been doing face painting, reply with a confident 'Oh quite a while now', even if it's only been a couple of months.

Another classic issue is after you have painted all the children at the party Mum will ask if you can hold on for a few moments longer as she's still waiting for another little boy to arrive who will definitely like his face painted. So you sit there and you wait for 10 minutes, and you wait for another 10 minutes ..... and then eventually this late-comer arrives. He's begrudgingly dragged over to the face painting table, and Oh what a surprise – he doesn't want it done because he hasn't settle into the party yet! This isn't a problem to stay for an extra 20-minutes or so if it's still within your booked out time-scale but it can mess up your day and subsequent bookings if it's not. When the customer makes the booking ensure that the time she has booked you for, will be for when all the children are in attendance.

You'll find that when you're painting at birthday parties, the children will keep returning to you for their lip-paint to be re-touched, or to sort out any smudges. You will need to use your judgement here as to how much time you're prepared to spend doing face paint touch-ups. Do you want to spend another 20 minutes correcting tear-stains and smeared mouths of every child that you've already painted? If the birthday child is asking for a re-paint then I will always, always do them. After all – it's their special day (and they're usually the ones who've had a cry because they didn't win the party game).

There are a hundred and one other things that I could go into with regards to event protocol for parties, but we'll leave it here for now as over time you'll start to put your own policies into place as your own experience grows.

School Fetes – These are usually booked through a member of the fete committee or someone from the schools' governing body and you will need to contact the school and ask for the name and telephone number of the person who is organising the school fete so that you can contact them to put yourself forward. When you eventually get to speak to the organiser it's also worth checking that you will be the only person face painting as fetes are not big enough for you to have competition there as it will have a drastic impact on your earnings. You need the monopoly, the sole concession.

The busiest times for school fetes are between May to July for the summer ones and between late November to the middle of December for the winter ones, and are run over a 2-3 hour time-scale. Plan well in advance when booking in your fetes, at least 10 weeks prior, and be picky about where you will go and that way you may find that you can book in a morning fete and an afternoon fete on the same Saturday.

We love the outside summer fetes best as there is plenty of room to manoeuvre and plenty of room for your queue to form. Indoor winter fetes can be a bit squashy and pushy and people become reluctant to queue because there just isn't the space (or the stall-holder next to you gets all stroppy because your queue is blocking their wares).

You can find out about local fetes in your area by visiting the events section of individual school websites or by typing a keyword-phrase search into your browser. Keep your eyes peeled for banners that will go up promoting the fete at the entrance to schools along with looking in your local newspaper for coverage on them.

To attend you will pay a small fee known as a table-top rent, which can be anywhere between £10 - £20 and generally paid out about 6-8 weeks in advance to the school. You may be fortunate enough that the organiser just agrees to take a commission of say 10% from your takings on the day, which is usually the cheaper option for you. Sometimes the organiser will ask you for a prize donation to be put into the raffle. You can print out a nice gift voucher for this purpose giving the recipient of your donation a discounted price off a local face painting party.

The price you charge for your service is dependent on how much you'd like to earn over the two to three hour time-scale, however what you'd like to earn and what you actually get doesn't always go hand in hand! As a rule we like to charge between £2.50 - £3.50 per face, however by charging at the higher price you will get comments such as 'No that's too expensive'. People are used to having teachers run the face painting stall at school fetes charging 50p to £1.00 per face and when a company comes in to provide the same service they expect you to charge the same price – which clearly isn't going to happen, because after all it's not the *same* type of service!

Sometimes the first 15-20 minutes of the school fete can be a little slow for you as people are just sussing out what's there and asking the children what they'd like to do first. However, before long you will start getting a queue which will grow and grow, and before long you'll find that the fete is coming to a close and you'll be the last one still working, way over time.

Village Fun Days – These are very similar to school fetes however they can last for up to eight hours. You'll see them advertised as Fun-Days, Community Events and Village Fayres. To find out where these events are taking place you can search the 'What's on' section of your county council's website, read local newspapers and community magazines, you can do an Internet search using a variety of keywords and keyword phrases and again by keeping a close lookout for any signage that is being displayed in your area.

The fee you will pay for these types of events can range from £50 - £100 per day for a 3mtr x 3mtr trade space which is the size of a standard gazebo.

Contact the organiser of the event well in advance, about three months before its taking place as this will give you a better chance of getting in before anyone else does. On that note you will need to clarify as to whether you have sole rights meaning you'll be the only face painter in attendance or will they be allowing more than one. This is where it gets tricky, very tricky, as risk calculations need to be put in place such as: What is the expected crowd attendance, are they promoting and advertising their event well, if you worked non-stop is that enough to cover your costs (trade stand rent and fuel as a minimum) and earn a good days living, is there any other local event taking place that could have an impact, is it going to rain, are you going to be tucked away down the bottom of a trade aisle that no-one will see. And that list could go on and on. As an example I won't attend a small community event like this where there will be another face painter if the expected attendance is less than 10,000 people. I will ask for sole concession and agree to pay a higher trade rent for the privilege. If the attendance is 15,000 – 25,000 people then I'm happy for another face painting company to be in attendance as long as we are competitive with our price indications, meaning that I'm not charging £4 per face and the other person is charging £2 per face – it must be fair competition with both artistes charging the same. Unfortunately in our industry most people will chose price over quality on the showground as the kids just want a bit of face paint on, and that is regardless as to how experienced you are, how artistic your work is, how professional your gazebo looks and what professional brand of products you're using. If the Charity face painters are there on mass charging 50p per face using cut-out photos from the Internet that is clearly not their own work– then you've had it, coupled with the fact that it's raining, you might as well go home and calculate the loses you've just made.

On the bright side though there is very good money to be made from the small community event if all the factors are in your favour and it's not unusual to be able to earn over a couple of hundred pounds for one day's work after all your costs have been taken out. So take a calculated risk when booking this type of event and if you get it right time and time again then this will have a massive impact on your earning potential and will be a huge success for your face painting business.

Shows and Festivals – This is the big one and not to be ventured into light-heartedly. You'll need a nerve of steel and a strong backbone (not just a wishbone) to attend these larger than life events. Over the year they'll cost you a small fortune but the earning potential is absolutely massive, and that all comes with a huge risk that again needs to be fully calculated.

Country Shows and Festivals of all kinds (pop, seafront, balloon, etc.) can be sourced through directories such as The Showman's Directory which is produced by Lance Publications on a yearly basis. In here will be complete listings of all the large events taking place across the UK from January through to December. The good thing about this directory is that it indicates the attendance for each show (based on the previous year's attendance) along with full contact details and web addresses so that you can easily get hold of the organisers. You can then go online and print off your trade stand application forms and send in immediately with your cheque to cover the rent.

Shows of prestige standing with large crowd attendance do however demand, and rightly so, very high rents. It's quite normal to pay between £300 - £600 per day for a 3mtr x 3mtr trade stand, yes that's per day, for the privilege of being there. So a 4 day event could cost up to £1200 in rent alone. We do find it amusing at this type of event as the general public seem to think that it's free for you to be there and you're just some kind of traveller who's rolled onto the showground with no regard to the logistics that it takes to actually attend this type of event. That's when you hear the usual comments of 'She must be raking it in'. Oh if only they knew! If you decide you'd like to do the large events you need to be aware that most rents need to be paid in January/February which will be months in advance and if you intend in doing a lot of these then you could be spending many, many thousands of pounds out at the beginning of the year. You need to have a very healthy bank balance to start with to be able to do this. Mimicks spent the first 16 years attending the largest shows and festivals across the length and breadth of the UK and as each event came and went I systematically put the trade rent back into a savings account so that at the start of the following year all my rent was readily available for me to write out the huge cheques that were needed for that season.

Now on to the up-side. Large shows and festivals have immense earning potential as long as the expected crowd attendance comes along, it's not raining continuously for the duration, you are one of only a few competitive face painters, there are no charity or free face painters and that you have prime position on the showground so that you can easily be found and have a constant footfall past your stand. You might be thinking here well how can I earn really good money if it's only just little old me painting as I can only physically do so many faces in a day. Absolutely. This is where you will need to either employ additional staff to help you or ask another couple of established face painters if they'd like to come along and share the costs. Days can be long as well as some events can stretch over a twelve hour period which is exhausting and back-breaking. At the large events that we attended, along with me and Ashlea, we also had four to five other employed staff members to make up our team. This way revenue could be capitalised on to make the maximum amount possible. But ..... of course it had a down-side. If it rained and hardly anyone came to the show we still had to pay the staff.

The other costs and logistics to take into consideration is how far you are prepared to travel. Some of our events would take us 6-hours to get there, so coupled with the fuel costs it also means adding on an extra two days for travelling purposes (and staff need to also be paid for that). Luckily we had a 6-berth motor home and additional tents for us to stay in so we didn't need to pay out for accommodation, but we had very little in the way of home comforts.

When attending shows and festivals you will sign a terms and conditions document which will outline all the instructions to be followed when on-site that have been laid down by the organisers and health and safety officials. This will include vehicle movement and trade parking details, set-up and break-down restrictions (you're not usually allowed to break-down until the show has finished) and trading times. Included in your contract will be all the necessary health and safety checks that will be enforced by the environmental health officers, trading standards and licensing officials. Sometimes you will be required to provide details of the flammable materials that have been used for your stall/gazebo, and other times you'll need to provide an in-date fire extinguisher and certificate. It will also go into detail regarding disposal of waste, emergency procedures to follow with regards to incidents, accidents and evacuation procedures and they will want to know how you intend to weight down your trade stall on grass or on hard-standing.

As I've said before I spent the first 16 years of my face painting business attending a different show every weekend from April through to September, and I loved every moment of it (well almost) and I wouldn't have changed it for the World. Poor Ashlea often reminds me that she spent most of her teenage years in a different field in a different part of the country. Even now when I visit a large event I'm transformed back to those days by the wonderful smells and sounds, the noise of the generators, the people, the atmosphere and the fun of the showground. Great times!

Corporate and Promotional Functions – This is by far the best type of event to do as it's the most fail-safe. It's a win-

win situation. These are companies running an event (indoors and outdoors) who would like a face painter to attend their venue at places like supermarkets, shopping centres and retail outlets, for promotional and entertainment purposes. Companies will also hold or sponsor village fun days and other community events and are happy to pay you to attend so that you can then face paint the public for free. Another good corporate booker is those in charge of organising student events, university balls and nightclub owners, etc. Large corporations will also book you for their Summer Bar-be-que parties that they're putting on for their staff or for a Christmas party they're organising for their staff and families. In fact the list is quite endless - from the smallest of companies to the larger blue-chip ones, they all love to book a face painter.

Unlike the above events that I have just covered whereby you take a certain element of risk, there is no risk when a company books you to attend their event as the corporate booker pays for the face painter to be in attendance for a set fee over a pre-set duration. This is the ideal situation as you will have guaranteed earnings regardless of how many people attend the event, what other entertainment activities they're providing and of course whether it's raining or not. Face painting is then provided for free or the booker might ask you to collect a small payment or donation from each person painted which then goes back to the company to off-set their costs to you.

Corporate bookers will request that you arrive in plenty of time to set up your work area before the face painting activity is to take place, even if that means that you have to stand around for awhile before the event starts. They will also expect that your standards are professional and that your appearance is presentable and that you should co-operate at all times and must not misrepresent the company in any way. A terms and conditions contract will usually be put in place by the booker for you to sign prior to the event taking place so they know that everyone will be singing from the same song sheet.

Because this event is classed as B2B (business-to-business) everything about the whole experience must be completely well-organised right from the very beginning, by you the face painter. From the first initial enquiry by the booker you must be very professional and be extremely knowledgeable about the service that you can provide for them. First impressions count and the booker will more than likely be contacting a few other face painters as well as you to get quotes for their event. Once booked, the paperwork that you send out to them – booking confirmations, contracts, terms and conditions, invoices - must be faultless in every way. From the moment you arrive at the event you'll be under scrutiny by the corporate booker. They'll be looking at things like how you set up your work area and display your menu board, how you interact with the public especially the children, are you open for business and not sitting down at your work station picking your nails or using your mobile phone. Even if it's quiet and you have no customers in your queue you should be standing up, talking to people as they pass and inviting them over to see what you can do for them. We're in an entertainment industry – so entertain! When you vacate the event it's also very important that you leave the venue exactly as you found it. So if tables and chairs have been bought over for you, offer to take them back at the end of your session. Always wipe down tables of theirs that you've used with a surgical spirit spray and pick up any pieces of paper or litter that may have been dropped on the floor.

Your enthusiasm, customer care and proficiency will go a long way and if you're seen to be providing an excellent service that the corporate booker expects, and has paid for, will help to secure any future bookings with them and of course being recommended by them to other companies. The majority of the work that Mimicks Face Painting does now is the corporate kind as it's a guaranteed income and anyway I'm all burnt out from the showground circuit!

Entertainment Agencies – Agencies and event planners are another really good area in which you should pursue. To be 'on the books' of an agency will help you to secure more corporate bookings as above, except that this time there is a middle man. The agency will do the leg-work so to speak and they will be the mediator between you and the corporate booker, and you will be responsible to the agency not the booker.

Search the Internet for the different types of agencies in your area and use search terms such as entertainment agencies, promotional agencies, event planners and wedding planners to name but a few.

It's a good idea to have a different rate-card for agencies as you want to give them your best price. So by shaving off a few pounds (up to £20 of the total price) from your corporate rate-card will help you to win the contract. This is because the agency will need to add on their commission, and if you're quoting them the same price as you would for a corporate booker by the time the agency has added on their commission you will probably be too expensive and have out-priced yourself.

When you are doing an event for an agency they generally ask you to conform to a no-self-branding disclaimer. This means that you will be unable to hand out any of your leaflets or business cards or have your company name displayed anywhere, which goes without saying. What they will expect is for you to completely promote the agency and any enquiries for business that you get must be referred back to them. By not stepping out of line here and by being compliant to their request, they will be more than happy to use you again in the future. Contracts will be issued to you at the time of booking which you'll need to read through and signed for that you acceptance their conditions. Get yourself on the books of as many agencies as you can and watch your business fly.

Charity Events –You'll have many, many phone calls from Charities that are organising their own event and are in need of face painters. But what they want are Free Face Painters.

They'll phone you and tell you how marvellous their event is going to be (that's their opinion), how many thousands and thousands of people are going to be there (prove it), how they're all going to want to be face painted (I don't think so), how great it's going to be for you to promote yourself (I can manage that on my own in other ways thank you), they've seen your work and think you're amazing and only want the best at their event.... and here's the crunch, they want you to take time out of your busy Summer schedule and attend for FREE, along with being privileged to pay them some commission on what you earn!

Now you never know from that one phone-call, but this in fact could be a great opportunity for you. It might be a fantastic event with a large footfall, the sun may be shining, you might have prime position, you're the only face painter, you may give out loads of leaflets and get many enquiries from that, the people have money to spend and you take a fortune and you only have to pay back a small commission which is so much cheaper in comparison than trade-rent.

Really! Again another calculated risk to put in place here. Do you agree it's going to be an amazing profitable event? Can your bank balance afford to make a loss? Is there another event you could be doing instead that has no risk like a corporate event or birthday party? Are you willing to try it out this year because it might just be good for you?

By accepting this type of event and logging it in your diary means that if a corporate booking comes in you'll need to refuse it as you're already booked out. You'll be turning away reliable income. I'm not saying for definite here that it'll be a waste of time as over the years I've attended Charity events whereby I've made a decent profit. They are far and few between however, and it's a decision that you'll need to make for yourself as and when the time comes.

When this type of enquiry comes in we explain our situation saying that it's too much of a risk for us to attend with so many factors to consider and that we need to earn an income, after all we're running a business. We then offer to attend on a paid corporate basis but offer them a good discount off our hourly rate because they're a charity. We also explain that they can then charge people to be painted which will help them to off-set our fee.

Some you'll win at, some you'll lose – swings and roundabouts.

So those are the types of events that you will be looking to do during your face painting career. Maybe you'll just decide to do parties and a few village fun-days in your first year of trading to test the water and see how you get along and then over time you may decide to venture out into the large showground world – but either way make sure you are clear on your outgoings, expenditures and charges and of course the logistics that will ultimately surround each event.

CHAPTER 6

Maintaining Industry Standards

Workplace Set Up

We've talked about the types of events that you can do, and next we will discuss how you can maintain the industry standards that are paramount to your success as a conscientious face painter with regards to your workplace set-up.

Without a completely organised, orderly, well stocked and efficient set-up you could be faced with an unpleasant working environment, and coupled with the frenzy of the event, the viewing audience and the queuing customers will all add up to unorganised chaos! And you definitely don't want that.

Prior to attending any event your face painting kit should be thoroughly cleaned and sterilised as explained in the 'Products and Equipment' chapter to follow later and packed ready for the next session which will include topping up of any necessary items that have run short.

Your work area needs to consist of a sturdy table that is large enough to fully lay out all your products and equipment onto that will be needed for the face painting session. For a professional and neat look it's a good idea for your table to have a floor length tablecloth as this is where kit boxes, handbags and coats can be stored underneath to prevent any of the general public slipping or tripping over these items if they're left out in the middle of the room.

If you can try to set your face paints out in the same order of colour sequence at every event. This way you'll get to know where your colours are positioned every time, as set out on the table. This may seem a trivial system to adopt, but it will save time as habits are made by doing just that. This same practice also applies for all other pieces of equipment, if they're laid out in the same place and order each time it will make for a very efficient working practice. All of the products that are needed to complete the designs on offer must be ready to hand as it can be very off-putting to the customer if half way through their application you have to rummage through your kit box to retrieve items such as gem-stones that you forgot to lay out in the first place.

On top of your tablecloth a towel should be placed which is used to press out your damp sponges in order to obtain the correct consistency of paint and water. Your towel by the end of the session will be quite multi-coloured as it would have been used to press out sponges and wipe away any excess paint from over-loaded brushes many, many times. Towels and tablecloths are easily washed in the machine and generally all paint marks will be removed by doing so.

Your customers chair should be positioned so that when you're working on them your product table is to the side of your working hand. If this simple step isn't taken into consideration when setting up your face painting station then you'll need to stretch across yourself and your customer to reach your products and equipment which along with bad practice can also lead to posture problems, which you won't want.

We do work in quite a 'mucky make-up' situation, and sometimes your work area can look a little bit untidy, to say the least. As long as you impose a strict discipline on yourself regarding cleanliness and orderliness your work area can remain an efficient and uncluttered face painting station. To keep it looking clean and tidy always dispose of waste immediately and never leave used baby wipes and cotton pads lying around on your table. Change your brush water as often as you can, approximately in between every 15-20 customers. We have an empty water container that our dregs are tipped into and a large bottle of fresh water for topping up our cups. Keep lids on glitter pots to prevent the wind catching them and blowing fairy-dust into your paints and have some spare sponges so that you can intermittently wipe over your paints if they start to look a little muddy. You should under no circumstances eat from your work station. Food and make-up don't mix well. Crumbs from sandwiches, biscuits and crisps can easily fall into your paint which will cross-contaminate them and if left bacteria will grow and multiply. Always take a lunch-break well away from your work area. You also need to be very diligent if you are going to have hot tea or coffee on your table (not particularly advisable) as it poses a huge risk in being knocked over onto some poor child's leg or you might be tempted to put your brush into it thinking it was your water cup. It happens!

A clean, tidy and organised work area is a very efficient work area.

To protect your customer from any accidental paint smudges from your sponge or brush you can use a shoulder make-up cape for this purpose to cover their clothes. We don't tend to use head-bands as they take too long to put on each customer, or we forget to take them off and you run the risk of head-lice re-allocation as well. It's far easier to clean your hands afterwards if you notice that a child has head-lice.

As well as making a good first impression you also need to be making a good lasting impression. Face painters usually have long queues with many family members waiting in line. If there is no other immediate entertainment happening then the people in line will have nothing more to do than watch you. It's at this point that you will be under close scrutiny by those who wait in line. They'll be looking at everything – your work-area set up, does everything look clean and hygienic, your display board, is it tatty, they'll be checking you out, do you look and act in a professional manner. You need to tick all the boxes because the people waiting in line are your prospective customers and you want them to see what a superior service you offer. By setting-up a professional work area that has an order of calm about it rather than looking like a chaotic jumble sale mess, and with kit boxes stored out of the way and out of sight, you'll be able to provide a first-class service to your customers.

Organisation of The Work Area

Prior to the commencement of your face painting activity you will need to ensure that all the following are in place, of which some of the points go into further detail in the Legislation and Standards chapter to follow:

- An organised and well stocked work area with the necessary products and equipment to provide the service as displayed, along with a supply of baby wipes or facial cleansing wipes
- Protective coverings for the work area such as tablecloth and towel
- Suitable chair(s) for the customer to sit upon
- A receptacle for the disposal of waste and used cleansing wipes
- A display board depicting the range of face painting designs that are on offer at the session
- A clear sign with the business/face painters contact information on which is a standard and legal requirement
- A clearly marked pricing structure
- A health and safety disclaimer informing customers of the contra-indications that will prevent or restrict the face painting application taking place, and what should happen should a child become distressed during the make-up application

- An optional rows of chairs for queuing customers to sit on
- An environment which protects customer safety
- A system for taking money, giving out change and storing takings
- A fresh supply of water for the face painting water cups
- A large empty bottle for discarding used water from the face painting water cups

As well as all of the above it will be good practice for you to also have:

- Business cards
- Leaflets
- Allergy intolerance forms
- Internet and photographic release forms
- A risk assessment
- A camera to record works of art
- The bookers information to hand
- Product ingredient checklist

Professional Appearance

Face Painting is very closely allied to the beauty industry and now there are specific City & Guilds and VTCT qualification units that can be awarded as a Level 1 and a Level 2 certificate. Regardless as to whether you have a qualification from an awarding body like this or have been trained by a private training company, or are completely self-taught with no background in beauty, you must follow the usual industry standards relating to image as your normal practice.

This includes:

- Keeping your hair tied back and away from your face into a neat style. If you have long loose hair then you'll find that it will accidently dangle into the face paint which is totally unhygienic and could contaminate your products. Also long floppy fringes will impede the way you work and you'll find it a nuisance if you have to break-away from your painting to sweep your hair out of your eyes.

- Your hands should be cleansed as often as possible by using a baby wipe or an alcoholic gel. Face painting is a mucky business and you'll find that your fingers will end up looking pretty multi-coloured as your session progresses. It's also wise to remember that you are touching the heads of many, many people, which is a great opportunity for head lice to jump ship from one head to another, using your hand as transport. Bear this in mind when taking a lunch break – so wash your hands.

- Your fingernails should be kept short without extensions otherwise you run the risk of scratching your customer's face or head. Germs and bacteria will harbour under long nails which again isn't too good for cross-contamination. If you choose to wear nail polish I would suggest that it looks fresh – don't forget that you're being scrutinised and chipped nail polish always looks so unprofessional.

- Keep your jewellery to an absolute minimum. Mainly because again chunky fashion rings and bracelets could scratch your customer and long necklaces will just get in your way. Furthermore, jewellery also has the potential to harbour germs. You'll need to make your own mind up as to whether you will be wearing facial studs or not. They are considered to be undesirable especially from many corporate bookers and they may also cause alarm to small children that are being worked on.

- Over the years I've seen a fair few face painters who have paid no regard to their appearance. Dirty jeans and sloppy t-shirts or sweatshirts would have done them no favours in acquiring any future business. Ideally your work-wear should be clean and professional looking and you could even make it consistent with the colour of your branding if you can. Black is such an easy colour to wear, an easy colour to buy and an easy colour to wash and it can be dressed up to look really smart and corporate or dressed down for the showground. Some face painters adopt a specific company uniform and it can be in the form of a polo-shirt, sweatshirt or blouse with their logo printed on it. Your customers will be influenced by the way you dress.

- Ensure that your shoes have low heels because if you opt for standing to face paint then you need to be comfortable with your feet grounded flatly down as you may be standing for many hours on end. Ideally, as a beauty standard, shoes should be fully enclosed for hygiene reasons so the flip-flop or sandal is out!

- Due to the close nature of our work, personal hygiene is of paramount importance. There is nothing more off-putting than bad breath, smoky breath, stinky fingers or body odour. A light perfume or body spray should be worn and always have a packet of mints handy (not chewing gum though)!

Getting Your Timings Right

A good time management plan is essential for running a service-based business as you need to ensure that you arrive to your event well before your start time. There's nothing worse than arriving to the venue late, all hot and flustered, because your Sat-Nav took you off in the wrong direction.

We always make a point of calculating our travel time by adding on an additional fifteen minutes per twenty miles to ensure that we get there on time. You'll also need to add on extra time for any booking-in processes that will need to be done and of course setting up your work area. You'll probably also need five or ten minutes to compose yourself before the actual event starts. So for a job that is relatively close to you that you can travel easily to on a normal day in say twenty minutes, you may find you need to leave home an hour beforehand.

Other things to take into consideration are making sure your kit and equipment is packed and ready to go well in advance. You don't want to be rushing around at the last minute trying to pack things together or looking for your favourite brush. Also putting fuel in your car should be accounted for beforehand as you know that sometimes the garage forecourt can be choc-a-block and it's times like this that you always queue for the wrong petrol pump. Taking into account any suspected road works in the area and any other events that may be taking place such as football matches can all add valuable minutes onto your travel plans. So head-off with plenty of time on your side. If it's unfortunate that you do arrive late for your event you should always offer to make up the time by staying on later if that's possible or to reduce your bill to them – very generously though.

If the event you're attending is over a 4-hour timescale you will need to let the customer know at the time of booking that you'll need to schedule a break into your session. For longer durations you'll also need to advise them on how long you will be taking for lunch. Planning this sort of thing into your session is very important as you'll need to stop people from queuing up if a scheduled break is pending. I will be going into more detail in a little while on how to effectively stop the queue from growing.

You will unfortunately attend events that are really slow and it's a case of spot the customer. You may become bored, fed-up, tired or whatever – but if it's a corporate event and you're being paid to be there for a certain amount of time you should stay right to the very end of your contracted time. Try not to be seen clock-watching (or yawning for that matter) and only start to pack your products and equipment away after you have checked that no-one else would like to have their face painted and that your time is up. Obviously if the booker has said that you can leave early due to lack of custom then it's perfectly acceptable to do so.

The opposite end of that scale is whereby the event is really busy and it looks like you won't be able to paint all the customers within the contracted time. This is when you can ask the booker if they'd like you to stay on for some extra time so that you can continue to work. This can be a very good public relations exercise here as you may be in a position whereby you can offer an additional 30-minutes of service for no charge at all. This will go a long way in building your reputation. If you intend to be paid for the extra time then it's most important that this is clarified to you from the person who booked you as you don't want any discrepancies when it comes to invoicing them for services rendered.

Working With Others

There will be times when you are scheduled to work alongside other entertainers such as clowns, balloon modellers, magicians and the like. You'll need to comply with and respect the other professional trade and their craft and may be required to work in conjunction with their activity, which could mean that you may have a quiet spell when they are performing, i.e., Punch & Judy.

If you are working alongside another face painter at a paid corporate event it's the correct protocol to introduce yourself and your company and to take a look at each other's display board so that you are familiar with what each artiste is offering to the public. If you are both situated in the same location at the venue then you may also wish to discuss how the queue should form – will there just be one queue for both of you or will you both have separate queues. Lunch-breaks can also be discussed and arranged so that both of you are not away from your work station at the same time.

You may be booked to work alongside a charity or organisation that is collecting donations for the face painting activity. If this is the case then you will need to clearly explain to the charity worker any details regarding your processes such as health and safety information, queuing procedures and any other applicable information that they can pass on to your prospective customers.

Always show a professional willingness to work cooperatively with others, and this will also go a long way in building your reputation. You could even go as far as exchanging business cards so that future referrals and recommendations can be made. I always take a card from any entertainment specialist who in my mind has provided an excellent service and I'm then able to recommend them to corporate bookers when they ask if I know of 'any good balloon modellers', etc.

Event Protocol

Having systems in place for an efficient working practice will ensure that you'll get asked to attend events and parties again and again and with a good code of behaviour on how you act and deal with the public during your time spent with them will all go towards growing a successful business.

Firstly, as discussed above, you must always attend the event on time – generally well before the activity is due to start so that you're ready and open for business when the time comes.

If you can arrive and be ready at a birthday party ten minutes before-hand then this will give you time to paint the birthday child before her friends start to arrive. This way he/she is ready to receive her guests (and the present of course) as they enter the room and it'll mean that you won't have to deal with painting a child who is becoming distracted with each and every ring on the doorbell! At parties you'll quite often find that what you paint the birthday child as, most of the others will follow suit, so you could end up painting twelve or so Butterflies all in a row. When you've finished painting all the guests at a party it's imperative that you ask all the children who didn't participate in your activity if they'd like to be face painted before you pack your products away. Ensure that the party parent has seen you doing this so she is aware that all the children were given the opportunity to take part.

If you're attending an event such as a fun-day, show or festival where customers are purchasing your service on an individual basis as a pay-per-face (PPF), systems for taking money should be adopted right from the start. It's generally better to take payment prior to the face painting application than it is to take the money after the face painting has been done as quite often the painted child will be so intent on showing their parent their creative masterpiece that a minute can pass before Mum reaches into her handbag to find her purse to pay you! Multiply that by thirty times and you will have thirty extra minutes of unnecessary wasted time, and that's an awful lot of wasted time at a 2-hour school fete. The payment up front system works very well as people queuing will notice this procedure happening and quite often the child coming to you will have the coins already placed in her hand ready to pay you. So in a fraction of time and all at once you can ask the child what they'd like to be painted as, and as you hold your hand out in front of them and they'll say 'Spiderman please' as they drop the money into your hand. This can then be very speedily placed into your money bag that is tied around your waist or that is over your shoulder. An excellent system to adopt to avoid time-wasting.

Sometimes events can be quiet and the space in between one customer to another is long. This can easily happen at corporate paid events or PPF events. During these slow periods you should be stood up by your work station chatting away to all who pass by trying to entice them into having their face painted. This is definitely not the time to sit down and read a book or magazine, file your nails or text on your mobile. This goes without saying especially if the event is company paid meaning you would have been contracted to work a number of hours and even if no face painting is being performed you are still being paid by the booker to work, and that means promoting good customer service.

Finally with regards to event protocol you need to ensure that at the end of your session and after you have packed away your products and equipment the last thing that should be done is to put the venue back as it was found. This means putting any tables and chairs back where they come from if using the bookers furniture, removing any waste from the floor no matter how small and washing and cleaning any hand basins that were used for face painting purposes. By leaving the work area as it was found in the beginning will leave a good impression and will go a long way to ensure that you will be booked again for future events.

The Inevitable Queue

Next we're going to discuss something that I get asked time and time again about putting a system in place for the inevitable queue. How to form one, how to stop one mid-flow for taking a break and how to cut one off at the end of a session. This is where a good system really comes into its own.

Before you even pick up your brush to starting painting you should decide on how and where you'd like you customers to queue, as sometimes people have to experience a long wait until it is their turn. A short row of chairs for say four to six people to sit on which they then move up to the front in turn will help to indicate in which direction you would like the queue to travel. The negative side of having a row of queuing chairs for the children to sit on as they wait is that Mum's and Dad's will sit on them for 'a rest' which is clearly not the purpose that they are intended for. You could also try using a piece of carpet cut into a 2ft wide by 8ft length for the kids to sit on and move up in turn (this deters lolloping parents as well). This is also an easier option for you to transport in your car if chairs aren't available at your event for you to use. If working at a large event where you have other traders to your left and to your right you need to be conscious of the fact that your face painting queue can have a direct impact on their sales for the day, and they will not be very happy if they have your queue in front of them all day long! Try to ensure that your face painting queue is directed out in front of your work area if that's possible leaving the sides free from people just standing in line. This will give you happier neighbours.

Quite often a face painting queue can look extremely long and stretch back for some twelve metres. It doesn't necessarily mean that every single person in the queue is waiting to be painted as quite often the child who is waiting in line has a Mummy, Daddy, Nanny, Grandad and baby brother in a pushchair with them! That one family group can actually account for two-square meters and quite often if there are fifty people queuing it might only mean that actually only ten of them are customers! A comment that is heard quite often is "No you can't have your face painted - just look at that queue".

Now here comes the answer to the inevitable question – 'How do I cut-off my queue at the end of a company paid event, when my time is up'? Your queue will need to be 'cut-off' well before the contracted time for face painting is over and the best time to do this is approximately one hour before the end of your session. There are a number of ways that this can be done.

The one we use most of the time is to put one of our promotional stickers on every child or adult that wishes to have their face painted that is already standing in line. As you go along the queue 'stickering-up' those to be painted you'll also need to count how many waiting children there are. If you have stickered-up more people than you can actually paint in that remaining hour then you'll need to speed up so that you can get through them all. If you know that you are able to accept another say five or so to join the line then you'll need to keep a close watch, sticker them up too when you can and then close the queue after that. In order to be able to do this effectively you will of course need to know, or at least have a rough idea, of how many faces you can paint in an hour.

Closing the queue can be done by either shutting your display board, putting a sign up that says the face painting is closed and only those in the queue with a sticker will be painted or asking the last adult to politely inform any people who join at the back that the face painting is closed (which most people won't do for some reason). Unfortunately this is where it can turn a bit unpleasant to say the least. You will get those who will join the queue regardless and when challenged they say they've been there all the time (which you clearly know is a lie). You'll get those that will remark that you're shutting way too early as you still have an hour to go (they don't seem to see all the kids waiting in line that you need to work through) and there are those that will take a sticker off a child that's already been painted so they can join the queue. To combat that one we also paint a blue star on the waiting children's hand so if they haven't got a sticker *and* a blue star then they weren't in the queue when it closed, simple as that!

You could also try getting all those wanting face painting to sit on the floor in front of you with their parents behind, or getting everyone to hold hands in a circle completely around your work area. As an additional safeguard to prevent more customers queuing you can put away the display board so no more choices of face designs can be chosen, ask the last person at the end of the queue to hold a sign saying that the face painting is closed, or you can get the last child in the queue to pop on a high-viz jacket that states that they are the last person to be painted or ask for the booker/security guard to stand at the back of the queue to prevent others joining (which works a treat). You will of course get those few who try to push in and include themselves in the queue, and occasionally someone will moan loudly and complain about you, however if you have a system in place you need to be strict and enforce it.

There will be times unfortunately when a child will become very upset that they can't be painted because the queue has closed and you will hear loud sobs, stamping feet and protests (and that's just from the mother)! It is difficult in this situation and each individual face painter will need to have their own specific policy on what they do under these unpleasant circumstances. Sometimes you just can't win.

These are the classic and common remarks you'll hear, and my answers that I'd like to say, but hold my breath to:

"Look what you've done; now you've made her cry".
No you've made her cry by causing a scene and not giving her something else positive to go and do.

"I'm sure you can do just one more".
If I did every just one mores I'd be here until bedtime.

"The queue was too long a little while ago so I thought we'd come back at the end".
So you didn't want to do what everyone else has had to do to get painted – wait in line.

"I've been waiting in line for 2-hours already".
Err no I don't think so; you weren't there forty-five minutes ago when I closed the queue.

If the face painting session is going to be long over a number of hours then you should inform the booker on how many refreshment/toilet breaks you will need. As a guideline a ten minute break could be taken for every two hours worked. However if the event is only three hours long then a break shouldn't be necessary. The same system as above for halting the queue can be used when taking a break by putting stickers on the waiting children. Before you rush off a sign can be placed on your table or display board that clearly indicates what is happening, i.e., 'The Face Painter is taking a break and will be back in ten minutes'. It's a good idea to have a spare towel so that the work area can be covered over as in the absence of the face painter children do love to play with the paint, push their fingers into the pots, squeeze your sponges and puff out your glitter - if they can get their hands on it!

Queues forming at children's birthday parties are a slightly different matter. You know that you will have time to paint all the children in attendance but the kiddies don't know that. They've probably been conditioned to get in line for face painting and they will assume they need to do so at a party. Not the case. If this happens then no other activity like pass the parcel, musical statues and any other game that the party parent has organised will have any takers. You need to let the children know that you only need to have one person in the chair and two at the most waiting in line and that you'll call them over when it's their turn. The party parent might ask if you'd like her to do some sort of list or number sequence something that you can work through, but this doesn't work very well as you could spend a couple of minutes trying to locate the next child on the list which will be time wasted. So just opt for calling children over to you when you can see that you need someone to wait in your very small queue.

All good face painters, like all good barmen, should automatically know who the next person to be served is, and so with that in mind keep a careful eye on what's happening in line and who is the next one to be painted.

Influencing Factors

Like any business with a service provision, there are influencing factors that you'll need to take into consideration when face painting on the paying public.

- Quite obviously the first one is your product and equipment range. This should consist of as many colours as possible in order to complete a vast array of different designs. To have just a basic set of the primary colours such as red, blue, green and yellow along with black and white in a working kit isn't going to be enough variation to fulfil customer needs. The same thing applies for a brush range, as diverse brush strokes are needed to paint a variety of face painting design elements.

- You will need to be able to use suitable techniques to apply competent and fast flowing face painting designs and these are mastered over time through training, consistent home practice and working on as many customers as possible in order to build the skills and confidence necessary.

- The characteristics of the skin should be visually inspected prior to face painting commencement. Is the skin condition and skin type good to excellent and appropriate for the make-up application; if not is it contra-indicated, highly blemished or excessively dry in any way? We'll be going further into this subject in a later chapter.

- Age should not influence any particular face painting design, as in this industry almost anything goes. It's not unusual these days for someone of very mature years to participate in having their face painted at an event just as very young children, even toddlers, love the experience. Please note here that before painting the under 3's, your insurance policy should be checked regarding any specific age requirements.

- Is the skin tone and colour suitable for the face painting design that has been chosen by the customer? If the skin tone is very dark some of the pale colour face paints will appear chalky and blotchy on the skin as opposed to the effects that can be produced with bright and bold colour shades. If the skin is very pale and almost transparent, any paint applied to the face will have a dramatic colour-blast effect which could in fact alter the desired outcome for both the painter and the customer.

- When working on male customers' consideration needs to be taken into account for stubble and bearded areas and the design brief changed or adapted accordingly.

- The customer will expect a realistic outcome with regards to the face painting design and prior to painting there are a number of factors to take into consideration first. Is the design that the customer has chosen suitable for their age – if they are very young a fully detailed tiger face with a lot of colour blending to the base will be too difficult to apply so therefore a quicker and less detailed tiger design will be much more appropriate. Adapt your creativity to the age of the customer. Cost is also a factor here - if the face painting designs are displayed as a set price and only a simple quick version has been painted then the price should reflect this and be reduced accordingly.

- Sustainability and durability of the design will be influenced directly by the reason that the customer is having their face painted in the first place. At fetes, fun days, shows and festivals the customer accepts that the face painting design will look good and last for only a certain amount of time. If, however, the customer requires a design that will last under strong lights (such as an actor would) or that they are attending a fancy dress party and would like the make-up to be long-lasting then the design can be part painted in cream make-up and set with translucent powder to provide a more durable finish. Some artistes that paint full body designs will set their work with hairspray, but not on the face though. There are also some very good fixing sprays available on the market from cosmetic suppliers.

- How you set your price will be influenced by the type of event that is being attended. When attending a PPF (pay per face) event the cost of the trade space rent needs to be taken into consideration. If the fee is fairly low like that at a school fete then the price charged should be between £2.50 - £3.50 whereas a slightly higher rate can be charged at a Village Fun Day or Community Event. The price of PPF will go up substantially if you attend shows and festivals where the trade space rent is extremely high and it is not unusual to charge between £6 - £9 per face at these types of events. Sometimes the general public will question the high price, especially if their child was painted for a £1 at the local toddler group fete, as they think that the face painter just rolled up to the show, set up a stall, and is doing 'just a little bit of face painting' and charging astronomical prices. They think that the grass that the face painter is standing on is free and they don't understand the logistics and expensive fees that were paid to be there that surround attending such an event!

- Environmental factors such as the weather will have a substantial part to play when applying your face painting designs. If it's cold and damp as it generally is in the winter months your paints may appear very moist and soft in their pot and can sometimes have a wet film across the top of the product. Yellow pigments quite often seep out of pink paint and sometimes the pigments can separate which will leave a strong darker colour on the surface of the cake. The consideration to take here is not to add too much water to the product otherwise you will flood the colour and it will make for a very wishy-washy application. Once the face paints have been bought inside to room temperature they will harden up to their normal consistency and can even be placed in an airing cupboard to speed up the drying process. Because of this situation do not store face painting kits in cold damp rooms, especially outside. Very cold rooms or working outside at Christmas events can be a little bit difficult as it's hard to work with very cold hands and fingers. Fingerless gloves don't work here either. Also children may be shivering which makes the matter far worse.

In hot summer months the face paint consistency will be quite hard and firm and in extreme cases may even separate from the pot it's contained in. A liberal amount of water on the brush is required to mix the product into a soupy consistency that is best for free-flowing lines.

Windy weather can be a bit of an issue as well as it will play havoc with your customers hair as it whips across their face getting in the way of your face painting brush. A hair-tie will help to ease this situation.

- Lighting will also affect the outcome of your face painting design. If working in poor light, such as at a nightclub, it can sometimes be very difficult to actually see what is being painted due to influences of strobe and flashing lights. It's advisable to speak to the booker before the event to arrange that the face painting set-up is positioned where there will be adequate lighting. Bright light, especially direct sunlight at an outdoor event, beaming onto the customers face gives rise to the child or adult screwing their face up in order to protect their eyes from the sun. An awning of some sort should be used here and this could be an umbrella, a gazebo or even the shade of a tree. A word of warning here – a red gazebo or tent will totally distort the colour of the paints and all colours will appear the same with hardly any differentiation. White awnings work best.

Code of Conduct

How you behave and conduct yourself at your events will go a long way in building your brand and business image, which in turn will result in customer satisfaction and frequent bookings.

1. Arrive punctually to your events with a view to being too early rather than too late.

2. Always attend each event with a cheerful and friendly attitude and sustain a polite manner at all times. You should be honest and obedient and not act against the booker's interest.

3. Face Painters are booked as entertainers, so remember that you are performing at every moment. Your composure and facial expressions are constantly under observation from the crowd. Take pride in your work as this will reflect on the success of your business.

4. Never gossip with your customers or colleagues. Keep conversation light and cheery. Respect confidentiality at all times and don't speak negatively about other face painting competitors or allied entertainers.

5. Adopt a positive attitude at all times when working and use open and inviting body language. Maintain eye contact with your customers.

6. Keep in touch with the people who are waiting in line, as well as the customer you are working on. Make the entire experience a memorable one from start to finish.

7. When working on children, welcome them in an inviting way as some may be apprehensive. Be professional and confident with a relaxing manner. Always remember your 'smile' as you offer your service.

8. Should you need to refuse the face painting application due to a contra-indication, remember to be tactful as you do so as some children may become quite upset.

9. Be sure to 'cut off the queue' in an orderly and competently fashion. No one likes to be refused a face painting service, so make sure that the crowd knows that the end of the booking contract is near.

10. Express your gratitude to the booker before you leave making your final impression upon the staff and management a positive one.

CHAPTER 7

Customer Care
and Communication

Influential Interaction

How you interact with your customer will go a long way in building your business image. You should always welcome your customer with a smile in a very friendly and relaxing manner, remembering that the majority of your customers are 'little people' and some can be rather nervous about the prospect of face painting, especially if it's their first time. You can usually tell who the apprehensive ones are as they tend to cling onto Mummy or Daddy and can appear a little daunted about the whole thing. Even though the parents may want the child to be painted it's a good idea to actually ask the child if it's something that they would like to have done and to not to be influenced by a pushy parent. If the child is able to tell you the name of the design that they have chosen and is ready and willing to sit on your chair to be painted then that's a good enough indication that it's their choice. If the parent has to force the child onto the chair with bribes and what-not then it's best to say that you don't think that he/she feels like face painting today and to maybe try another time.

Some customers will approach your display board just to have a look at what's on offer. At this time you should give them any advice that they may require about your service. Usual questions at this point will be to ask how much it is, how long the face paint will stay on, and how to remove it when they get home.

Most parents and carers like to read out the choices of designs from the display board to their children. Occasionally parents will like to influence the choice of the face painting design for the child and an argument between them can happen, which I think is unfair. If the child has been given the go ahead that they can have their face painted, basically it should be their choice of which design they choose. Their face, their choice. If you hear that a child's choice of face painting design is being imposed, then you could always offer to paint the parent into what they so badly want for their child - most will then let the child choose for themselves! The same thing can easily happen with a group of lads. One of them will choose a face and sit in the chair to have it done and when his eyes are closed the other guys are encouraging you to paint something completely different like a sparkly fairy or something. In this situation it's best to go for what the paying customer has actually asked for to be on the safe side.

Customer Preparation

After welcoming your customer and taking the money for the service provided, ask what face design they have chosen to be painted as. Make sure that all the products and equipment that you need are on your workstation to save time rushing backwards and forwards to retrieve items.

Once the customer is seated ensure that they are comfortable and not leaning too far back in the chair as this will be awkward for them and it will put a strain on your back if you have to lean over to reach them. Some of the high chairs that we use as face painters, such as director's chairs, can have quite a large gap in the back and if you're not careful a small child could easily slip through. To prevent this from happening it's a good idea to make some sort of additional section that can be fixed in place on the open part of the chair to prevent this from happening. Even though the parent is in attendance whilst you're painting their child it will be your responsibility to ensure that they are safely seated and positioned correctly.

Visual Skin Inspection

It's most important to perform a visual inspection (MENS = Mouth, Eyes, Nose, Skin) on all customers prior to the face painting application taking place, checking for any contaminating conditions (contra-indications) that may be present. This will prevent your products and equipment from becoming contaminated by the passing on of any bacterial or viral infection from one person to another.

A visual inspection is simply undertaken in a quick and unobtrusive manner whilst asking the customer what they would like to be painted as. It's at this point that you will take a look at the customer's eyes, nose and mouth and also their skin to see if they are suitable to be worked on. The customer is unaware that this is taking place as it is a standard industry practice. Should you be concerned regarding any disorder that is present you should ask the customer or the parent/carer of the child what the visible condition is. At no time should you diagnose any condition presented to you as you are probably not a medical expert. In the beauty industry all clients that we work on will have a thorough facial examination and a skin analysis performed, but as a face painter we clearly don't have the time or resources to do that. Nevertheless it's still very important that we do undertake some sort of visual inspection and are competent enough to deal with our findings.

Beware The Bogeyman

Well not so much the bogeyman – but the child with candles that look like they are three days old, that the parent hasn't even noticed! Prior to commencement of the face painting design ensure that the face has been wiped over using a baby wipe or facial cleansing wipe to remove any dirt, oil or sweat and if necessary some children should have their noses blown as well (not by you the face painter though)! For this purpose you will need to have a large supply of wipes handy at all times. A lot of parents will do this for their child before they climb onto the face painters chair, however there are many, many parents who clearly don't look at their children when they are in the queue for face painting and you are presented with a child who has more tomato sauce and cheeseburger around their mouth than in their tummies or sporting a lovely thick ice-cream moustache!!!

After the parent has cleansed the child's face you will need to protect their clothing with an overall or make-up cape to avoid getting paint splashes and smears on their clothes. You can easily keep their fringe away from their face by sweeping it back with your non-working hand and this will also aid your balance. You can then proceed with your face painting application.

Correct Posture

It is important for you to maintain the correct posture during the face painting activity, and this not only applies to you but also for the customer you are working on. Face painting activities can take place over a number of hours and if the correct posture isn't maintained then back problems may occur.

If you choose to face paint standing up with your customer on a high chair then you'll need to stand with your feet slightly apart, distributing your weight equally between both legs to avoid repetitive strain on the pelvis. Where possible keep your back straight to eliminate pressure on the spine and to prevent fatigue in your upper back. This is my preferred method to work in as you have more control over your painting space as you can move with ease to the side of the customer to easily paint any out of reach areas.

If you opt to sit down to face paint with your customer seated directly in front of you then your sitting posture is equally as important. The child seated in front of you will need to have their legs positioned inside your knees and the two chairs will be pretty close together. Make sure that they are sitting upright in the chair with a straight back and not lolloping backwards. The further back into the chair that the customer is then the further you will need to stretch forward which again will put an awkward strain on your back and your upper arms. They need to have their head slightly turned upwards, their hands need to be positioned in their laps and their feet should be tucked in under their chair. You'll find that some children will want to swing their legs when seated and this should be discouraged as they'll be swaying all over the place.

It's not possible to work chair-to-chair like this with adults as you will end up the same height as the customer, and for an efficient face painting application you will need to be higher than they are. So when painting an adult you'll need to stand up to the space at the side of them. Adults legs shouldn't be crossed otherwise they will get in the way of you so ask them to tuck their legs under the chair.

Your products and equipment need to be positioned closely to your working hand, so if you are right handed then your work area should be set up to the right side of you. This will prevent you from stretching across your body with your working hand to reach all your bits and bobs.

Get your standing or sitting posture correct from the on-set and this will prevent injury and any long-term aches and pains.

Your Body Language

Your body language will play an important role on how you are being perceived by those around you with regards to non-verbal communication. You posture, your gestures, your facial expressions will all be observed by customers that you are working on, those in the queuing area and of course by the booker. Become aware of the signals that you are sending out that are shown by your body language.

Positive signals would include maintaining eye contact when communication with someone, smiling, having a relaxed posture, nodding in agreement, leaning slightly in towards the other person and mirroring their posture. Negative signals that you may inadvertently put out is yawning, frowning, turning your back intentionally on people, fiddling with something, having your arms crossed as this creates a barrier and clearly says don't come near me and leaning on your hand.

Studying other people's body language is a great thing to do as you can learn a lot from this. You can then decide for yourself whether what you see with regards to gestures, signals, and any other non-verbal communication should fit into the positive or negative attributes.

Speaking and Listening

Many customers are intrigued about face painting businesses and will ask you questions about how you came to be in the business, where were you trained and if you have a 'proper job' (funny but people don't think that face painting can ever be a proper job)! They will ask if you come to birthday parties and how much you charge, and they might even ask if you're available on such and such a date – so it's a good idea to take your diary with you to events so that you can take future bookings.

Customers will ask you how to remove the face paint and some may even ask what the product ingredients are. Other will ask what brand of paint you're using and compare it to cheaper brands that they have probably seen and even used themselves before. You'll get many of those that will say "Yeah, 'cos I do a bit of face painting as well"... and they'll proceed to tell you about how busy they were at their best-mates party. They may even like to tell you stories about friends of friends of friends who had a reaction to face paints recently and any horror stories they might like to elaborate on!'

They'll like to tell you that it's such a shame that you haven't got a mirror so that you can show their little girl afterwards, when you clearly have one on your table. Many will ask how much it is, even when there is a huge price sign displayed, and at the end of a very long day you'll get those that will ask if you can change a twenty pound note (I should think so at this stage of my face painting session).

Mums and Dads will ask their children if they'd like to be Pace Fainted and children will ask if they can have Pace Fainting. Classic!

Comments will be made by the general public that you will hear time and time again, hundreds of times over in fact! Always act as if they're the first person to ever make a quick-witted comment, such as "Can you make my wife look younger". People like friendly and pleasant communication and don't expect to encounter an abrupt face painter, so speak to your customers with enthusiasm and be very knowledgeable and forth-coming in all questions asked.

Speak clearly when communicating with customers and use related terminology that they will be able to understand. This is of paramount importance when speaking to very little children and it's a good idea to bend down to their level when talking to them. At the same time be a very good listener. Even though you'll only be with your customer for about five minutes, it's amazing how much communication can take place in that short time.

You should also make a point of being aware of the conversations that are taking place around you by the waiting customers as this can lead to a business opportunity that can be maximised on, so listen intently. There's more about this sort of thing in my other book 'Growing Your Face Painting Business'.

Working on Children

Some children find it hard to sit still for any length of time so by communicating with them and speaking reassuringly to them throughout the make-up application will help them to relax. You can talk to them about how good they're being and about how wonderful they'll look when it's finished. Talking them through the colours that are being applied will also help to help them settle. For the majority of customers it won't be necessary to hold a conversation with them as you work on them – and this is the ideal scenario as it's a lot easier and quicker to work on someone who is quiet and still as opposed to someone who is chatting away needlessly. You need to be aware of the mother who asks the child questions when the face painting is taking place. They will usually ask things to their child such as "Does it tickle" which inevitable requires the nod of the head or a spoken answer. If an answer to a question is imminent, it's best to move your brush away from their face and stop painting for a moment so that the child can answer the question. Mum will then usually apologise at that point for asking the question.

Sometimes parents ask if they can leave the child with you so they can wander off for a while. This is a no-no and totally discouraged as you cannot accept responsibility for the child and you are highly unlikely to be insured for this purpose. The parent/carer must be around at all times so let them know your policy should this situation arise. You will also find that children will wander up to your work station as the parent waits in the queue. Children should not come into your face painting area unsupervised as there is a very high duty of care attached to supervising children which is difficult to defend, so you'll need to call Mum over and ask her to keep her little one with her in the queue. Children waiting immediately in line will like to lay across your lap if you're sat down to see what you're doing so they can get a closer look, or they'll be standing behind you but will be leaning on your shoulders and bouncing around! Curious kids that are close to the front of the line won't be able to resist the temptation of 'having a play' with your stuff. They like to poke their fingers in your paint, squeeze your sponges and blow into your glitter pots. If you see this happening let the child know that you'll be unable to paint anyone who is playing around with your make-up. Children leaning on your table have a tendency to cough, splutter and sneeze all over your paint and when done with such force that runny green candles shoot out ..... that's when you think to yourself.... why on earth did I want to be a face painter!!!!

So when the child has gone through the queuing process and they are ready and waiting in your chair ideally you'll need them to close their eyes gently without screwing them tightly together. If a child being painted can't close his eyes without screwing them up, then unfortunately the whole of his face will be screwed up as well as having a scrunched up nose and a wide open mouth. A very difficult canvas to work on indeed. After explaining that you need them to close their eyes just like when they go to sleep, if they still can't get the hang of it then it's better to work on these children with their eyes open in order for their face to stay free from creases and wrinkles. You could also go as far to check whether adults are wearing contact lenses or not. If so then work very lightly on the eyelid as it can be a bit prickly for them.

Occasionally you'll find that some children my hold their breath for some reason or another. Let them know that we're not going swimming and they can breathe as normal. Children who are confident with face painting and have had it done many times before will just climb onto your seat, tell you what they want, close their eyes and be still as a mouse. They're great to work on and they'll end up with a flawless work of art.

Utmost care must be taken when working around the delicate eye area and it's important not to paint too close to the lash line otherwise you run the risk of the product flooding the lashes and entering the eye. It will also make it very difficult for the parent to remove if it has covered the lashes and some children have been put off face painting because they have had a bad experience in having it removed by their parent. Also if you were to paint say a batman face which can be quite black and you've taken this right into the lashes then Mum will have a very difficult time in removing it and poor little Johnnie will have to go to school the next day wearing black eyeliner. Not so cool!

Sometimes children and adults can become 'jumpy' when a wet brush is suddenly swept across their face as they didn't see it coming because their eyes are closed. You can let them know just before you place the brush on their skin that it's coming by resting your little finger on their face first, so as not to startle them.

Occasionally you'll have a child that becomes distressed during the face painting application for no reason at all. You didn't do anything wrong, they just had enough and fancied a little cry. In this case you should abandon the procedure immediately. Trying to console the child will generally makes matters worse and they'll cry even harder and the parent may even insist that you keep on going, sometimes even putting the child in a head-lock so you can do so. Explain that you can't paint a child who is clearly upset and obviously doesn't want it done, and who is being forced to sit still.

Showing your customer their face in the mirror after the painting is done will produce one of three reactions: Number one – no reaction at all. Totally dead-pan. They are probably studying what you've done to them or they don't actually recognise themselves. Number two – big smiles. They are clearly very happy with the result and love what you have done to them. Number three – cry. For no reason at all they burst into floods of tears. You haven't done anything wrong; they just got a little surprise (or fright) at what they now look like. At this point they will reach out to Mum for a cuddle and you need to be quick here to let the parent know that as the paint is still damp this may transfer to her t-shirt and leave a green monster imprint all over her lovely white top.

After the painting is finished and you've shown your customer in the mirror, and gauged their response, make sure that you can clearly see that the child has been reconciled with the parent. Some Mums and Dads step back a little when the painting is taking place and it can be a daunting prospect for a child when they open their eyes and they can't see any family member anywhere. Do not let a child wander off to look for them on their own, otherwise they might not be able to find them and they could end up getting lost in the crowd.

CHAPTER 8

Products and Equipment

What's Going To Be in Your Kit?

The market-place for everything face painting is so extensive these days unlike a couple of decades ago when I was just starting out and trying to source products and equipment for my new business. It was made even more difficult way back then as the Internet was in its infancy stage and most people didn't have the luxury of a computer let alone even knew what a search engine was.

Things have changed dramatically over the years and not only is it easy-peasy to find almost everything that your heart desires from sitting in front of a laptop, but these days you have so much choice with an amazing selection of top quality face painting products out there for you to choose from.

The great thing about this is that you now have choices; you can choose from a diverse range of face paints and build your kit according to your own preferences. Most face painters these days will use a variety of brands as loyalty over one particular make has shifted due to the fact that certain products produce certain results. Take black water make-up for instance. In order to paint clear and intricate lines and thicker bold lines you need a product that is absolutely jet-black that lasts the length of the stroke and doesn't end up producing a line that's wishy-washy and looks grey and transparent. There are a number of brands that do this superbly and of course there are also a number of brands that just don't come up to the mark.

Over time and as your experience grows you will no doubt find yourself buying a diverse range of face painting products that will be suitable for your needs. No two face painter's kits are alike as we all have our favourites that include likes and dislikes. It's all about having fun and playing around with not only paints but also brushes and glitter until you find something that works perfectly for you time and time again.

Water Makeup

Because you'll be using a diverse array of products and equipment you will be frequently asked by inquisitive customers about what you are using, so therefore product knowledge is of paramount importance. You will need to be aware of the basic ingredients of your particular brand as some customers may have a known irritant to an allergen. Ingredients, however, have not been included in the lists that follow as there are so many quality face paints on the market to choose from.

Your face paints (water make-up and aqua-colour products) are purchased in a compact cake form in pots ranging from 2.5ml to 90ml in size. This product needs to be diluted with water from the brush by mixing the product into a creamy and soup-like consistency. If too much water is mixed in to the paint cake then your brush stroke will be wishy-washy with no intensity of colour pigmentation and if not enough water is mixed in the brush stroke will drag and look patchy and be inconsistent in application.

It's for this very reason – the mixing together of water and product to make a workable consistency - that water make-up should be applied directly from its pot/tub as opposed to using a 'cut out or decanted' method which is a commonplace beauty standard. To cut out a small amount of say four to five colours for any proposed design and to place each one on a separate wooden spatula is neither cost effective nor time effective for the face painter. That's why it is so very important that you are aware of cross-contamination between person to product and you are totally clear on the skin conditions responsible in order to deliver a thoroughly safe and hygienic face painting application. Most water make-up products have an anti-bacterial agent added to them to help in prohibiting the growth of organisms, and as long as you have checked your customer and they are deemed suitable for the face painting application then it is very unlikely that cross-contamination will take place. Stringent policies must be enforced here by you.

Before choosing your brand to use you'll need to make sure that they have FDA and/or EU approval and that they are fit for their intended purpose. Over the years I've seen some really dodgy face painting applications where people have been using craft paint, watercolour paint and even acrylic paint. Recently there has been a spate of cheap face paints being sold in pound shops, and if you were to read the back of these packets it clearly says not to be used around the eyes or mouth area – so that's pretty obvious that they're not face paints. If you're going into business as a serious face painter it goes without saying that you certainly wouldn't make space in your kit for such a dubious item. So make sure what you're using is in fact face paint that has been approved and regulated. Some excellent brands to look out for are Grimas, Paradise by Mehron, DiamondFX, Cameleon, Superstar and Wolfe.

Once water make-up has been applied it is very quick drying and most of the better brands do not smudge on the skin surface once it has dried. The range of colours available is quite extensive as is a diverse selection of effects such as metallic, pearl and shimmer. Water make-up is very versatile and the colours can be mixed together to produce an exciting array of different shades and this can be done by mixing directly into the pots towards one side of the cake or on a mixing palette that you can purchase from a craft store. These days the product can be bought in a 'rainbow effect' of colours which are known as split cakes. These little blocks of multi-colours are a fantastic way for applying a quick base using a sponge for a butterfly or with a brush to create some amazing floral effects and the like. This product is a definite must-have to add to your kit. Split cakes are fairly easy to make by pressing small rolls of colours into a spare pot and pressing firmly into place, however because you have decanted the product from its manufactured pot you may have an issue with your insurance should a reaction occur as the product has not been used in its original form. So do think twice about decanting products into other pots.

Like I've said before each face painter has their own preferred brand and it's fair to say that most of them will have a kit that has a variety of paints and colours from a variety of the top leading manufacturers. You'll get to know what your favourites are over time but it's definitely well worth experimenting with as many as you possibly can. For intricate line work and fine details in white and black you will of course need a product that has a high pigmentation in order to get the depth of detail you require in face painting.

Face paint cakes, in their pots and palettes, must be thoroughly cleaned after each and every session. To do this, finely spray each cake of paint with a mist of distilled water and then wipe over the surface with a cleansing wipe which will remove any debris from the paint and will freshen up the colour again. Next use a clean damp cloth which has been sprayed with surgical spirit and wipe over the pot or palette that the cake sits in. Always store your products at room temperature and never leave them in a cold damp shed, the boot of your car or against a radiator. Your kit is now fresh, tidy and clean for your next face painting session.

Makeup Sponges

High density synthetic sponges are used in face painting as opposed to natural ones. High density means that the holes

116

throughout the sponge are very tiny which aids in the absorption of the water make-up which produces a better coverage over the skin producing a more flawless and streak-free finish. Sponges are usually purchased singly and are large and round and are very low cost indeed. We tend to cut most of our sponges in half as this then gives you a nice straight edge for applying base-work which needs a definite solid line that you can stipple (dab) on to create your desired shape. Latex sponges used in make-up applications are not suitable for face painting as they do not hold adequate product and will cause a smeared and streaking effect on the skin.

The other type of sponge you can purchase is a stipple sponge that has a large random weave and this is used for applying effects such as beard stubble or blood and bruising for horror and casualty effects. Another must-have for your kit, especially around Halloween. Also available are sponge daubers which are basically little sponges with a flat-top that are stuck onto a stick. This item is great in applying the perfect round shape needed to create effects such as spider body's, flower centres, caterpillars and painted on body jewellery.

After your face painting session your sponges should be washed at 40 degrees in a washing machine by placing them all into a cotton bag, a bit like a small pillow-case, and tying the top securely with a cord or rubber-band. Your sponges will come out of the wash perfectly clean with all the paint residue removed and will now be ready for your next face painting session. It's wise to remember here not to store any damp sponges in a sealed container as this will encourage any small particles of bacteria to multiply and grow into a forest! Once a sponge has become old and hard and has lost its springiness it should be discarded. Sponges are cheap, so throw-out and replace frequently.

A very controversial conversation that has been debated and discussed many times on the face painting forums is to whether you should use a clean fresh sponge on every customer. I do find this a little bit counter-productive because if you took that stringent measure then surely you would also need to have a clean set of brushes and a fresh water-cup per customer, along with a new set of paints probably! In the late 1990's we were attending some very large shows and festivals during the summer months and were painting some 300 customers per day, and over a 4-day event we would have needed to have taken over 1000+ sponges with us if we were to adopt this policy. As long as due care has been taken in cleansing the customers face thoroughly and checking for contra-indications before starting then we feel it's not necessary to use a clean sponge per customer, however this is left to the discretion of the individual face painter and whichever way you wish to go on this will be your decision. Saying that however, we do actually use one clean sponge per customer at the majority of our events now. Took a little while to get used to but it is working okay for us now and is a policy we are more than happy to adopt.

Brushes

There are many types of brushes available on the market which are suitable for face painting, ranging from synthetic ones to natural hair bristles. When choosing a brush to use you should test simulated strokes against the back of your hand to ensure that the bristles return to their former shape, i.e., are they springy and do they maintain their flexibility? A brush that is not strong and is too floppy will be unable to produce any good brush strokes. Also look for brushes that have tight compacted bristles as opposed to being fluffy and sparse on the tip. This will help to give you a more defined brush-stroke.

The favourite shape and style of brush for face painting is what's called a round brush. These have a long slim line and have a fine point at the tip. They come in a range of sizes right from 0 which would be used for intricate fine-lining through to a number 8 which will give larger coverage with your brush strokes. The firmer you press down with the bristles the thicker the stroke will be. As a guide a number 3 or 4 will be a good size to start with as you'll be able to create some very common brush strokes like teardrops, swirls and starbursts with these. Flat bristled and filbert bristles are good for covering large areas and block colouring.

Your brush is very important in face painting and if you have an unsuitable or inadequate one then this will drastically effect your design and application, so it's worth spending some money on a range of brushes to find the ones that suit your work best. Most suppliers of face painting products stock a good range of brushes and artistes brushes are commonly used in face painting and can be purchased from all good stores selling artist and craft supplies.

During your face painting session you should intermittently wipe through the bristles of your brushes with surgical spirit on a cotton wool pad to keep them as well sanitised as you can, and especially after painting the mouth area. You may however prefer to use a cotton-bud or a disposable brush for painting in the lip colour. After each face painting session the brushes should be washed in warm soapy water using a mild detergent or a baby shampoo ensuring that the entire water make-up residue has been removed from the bristles. You should then immerse them into a sterilising solution such as Milton for no longer than ten minutes and then left to air-dry.

Brushes tend to be one of the most expensive items that you will purchase, as it is a trial and error process finding the ones that are most suitable for your needs and you'll probably end up with more brushes that you don't like rather than those that you love. When you do find that ultimate brush that you love you'll become totally obsessed with it and will break out in a cold-sweat if you get to an event and realised you've left it at home!

Glitter and Gemstones

Care should be taken when choosing loose glitter to enhance the face painting design as metallic craft glitters are not suitable for use. A metallic craft glitter feels sharp to the touch when rubbed between the fingers. This is due to the particles being cut out in random irregular octagonal shapes that have sharp edges. Should these metal glitter particles enter the eye, mouth or lungs it could have a serious consequence of scratching and causing an open would which could give rise to an infection taking hold. Never use craft glitter in any face painting applications even though they are really cheap to purchase.

Cosmetic glitter on the other-hand is suitable for face painting as it is made from polyester and soft to the touch due to being cut from rounded disc shapes which will not cause any scratching if entering the eye, mouth or lungs. Polyglitter is generally very sparkly and is available in a huge variety of colours to compliment your face painting designs. The best choice to use if you're only going to purchase a few is gold, silver and iridescent as these will coordinate with anything. Loose glitter can be applied with your ring-finger to a damp base as this will give it extra staying power and you can then paint in your line work over the top. If you apply loose glitter with your finger at the end of the painted design you'll need to make sure that your lines are dry so as not to smudge your work. Glitter is also available in a puffer bottle which is great as it also puffs out over the hair and onto the customer's shoulders, making a very pretty and sparkly effect. You can never have enough glitter I say – mind you I'm a bit of a glitter junkie.

Another popular glitter application is to use a product called liquid bling which is used for fine outlining and looks fantastic when applied to the outside edges of flowers and swirls and also used to make small sparkly dots. This item comes in a selection of colours to enhance your artistic creations.

Gemstones and sequins are available for additional enhancement. Craft stores supply gemstones that have a peel-off pad with a glued back surface to the stone which make for a fast application to the design. If the gemstone or sequin needs to be attached with the aid of skin glue, then a water soluble spirit-gum can be used for this purpose. Take care if using false eyelash glue as some customers may have intolerance to latex products. Prior to any type of glue application always check that the customer has no known allergies to any type of glue adhesion.

Transfers and Stencils

Most face painting designs are done freehand without the use of a stencil; however mini stencils are now available in a huge range to enhance your face painting or body painting application. They are small enough to hold in place over the features of the face with one hand as you dab on a contrasting secondary colour from a sponge held in your other hand. Monster faces can be brought to life and made more realistic when a pre-cut stencil is used across the forehead area to create some interesting scale effects and your fairy princess face design can be jazzed-up using a pretty floral or swirls stencil on the cheekbones.

When applying painted tattoos or motifs to the arms or legs you may need some guidance or assistance in the beginning, maybe a little bit of cheating which isn't a bad thing! To make a transfer which is transferable to the skin there is an easy and cost-effective method to use. Take a small piece of tracing paper and trace over the design you'd like to replicate using a copy pencil, also known as a magic pencil or hectograph pencil (the sort that tattoo artist's use which is safe for the skin). Never use a lead pencil straight onto the skin as it can be harmful. Next take a dampened cotton-pad and press it onto the skin where the transfer is to be placed. Make sure that you hold the pad over the area of skin for a while to make the surface of the skin quite clammy rather than wet. Make sure that the skin is damp and tacky and not too wet otherwise the copy pen will not penetrate through the water barrier that is sitting on the skin.

Place the transfer onto the damp skin with the copy pencil outline facing downwards and using the damp cotton pad rub firmly over the back of the tracing paper. Generally the blue colour of the copy pencil will turn darker through the tracing paper meaning that it has transferred sufficiently. Peel the transfer off slowly and you will be left with the outline of your design which is now ready for you to paint in using your water make-up.

Choose designs that you wish to copy that have solid outlines, such as flowers, hearts, butterflies, spiders or snakes, etc. You can take inspiration from children's colouring books, storybooks and vector images on the Internet. Transfers are great to use for arm tattoos or body painting designs and can also be used for free-hand glitter tattoos or henna bodyart. If you know that you're going to have a run of a particular motif then you can pre-draw your transfers out at home onto tracing paper and store them in envelopes ready for immediate use.

Effective Removal and Aftercare Advice

Your customers should be advised on the basic steps of removal. Face paint can be easily removed by using a couple of methods and advice on removal should always be given to the parent/carer. The easiest way to remove all traces of the make-up is to use facial cleansing wipes or baby wipes – the former being gentler on the skin. Another good choice is liquid soap or a baby shampoo which can be done during the child's bath-time if necessary. This can also be a fun factor as they can watch the lathery bubbles change into a variety of multi-colours! Remember to make it easy for parent removal by not painting too close to the lash-line as the face paint will quite easily flood the lashes and Mum will have a job removing it all. Excessive use and rubbing with baby wipes can cause irritation, so advise the customer to use them sparingly. I always let my customer know that if baby wipes with Aloe Vera are to be used to remove the face paint, then this will give off a 'smelly egg' odour (sulphur smell) as the paint and Aloe Vera begin to react together! Not nice!

When the skin is clean and all traces of the face paint have been removed it is advisable to apply a small amount of moisturiser which will have a soothing and calming effect on the skin as it may feel a little dried out after the face painting application has been removed.

Your Perfect Kit

So your perfect kit will include all the product and equipment items that I've listed below, all packed nicely into a kit box or kit bag:

- Table and chair
- Tablecloth and towel
- Face paints – matte, metallic, pearl and shimmer
- Water cups
- Water bottles – one with clean water and an empty one for used water
- Brushes in a brush caddy
- Glitter – loose, puffer and liquid
- Gemstones, sequins and water soluble spiritgum
- Stencils and pre-made transfers
- Sponges – high density, stipple effect and daubers
- Sponge containers/bags – one for fresh sponges and one for used sponges
- Water dispenser or spritzer-spray for dampening sponges
- Baby wipes and alcohol gel
- Mirror
- Surgical spirit
- Cotton pads, cotton buds and disposable lip brushes
- Waste bin/bucket/bag

There will of course be other additional items that you'll choose to have in your perfect kit which will also include all your promotional material, display menu board and sales literature.

The Face Painters Display Board

Over the years I've seen many different ways that face painters have used to display their artistic creations from hanging photos in plastic wallets and sticking them to the sides of their gazebo with parcel tape to fabulous floor to ceiling exhibits. How you choose to display your menu of designs will all depend on your budget and of course your available time to create one. Most face painters have their work printed on card which is then laminated to protect against the elements and you can easily fit 2 face designs onto an A4 sheet. Your local print shop will be able to laminate for you if you don't have your own machine (something worth investing in though). The good thing about these display cards is that you can easily change your menu to suit the seasons, such as Christmas, Easter and Halloween if you stick them onto your board with blu-tac.

Ideally your display board will need to be correctly positioned within your trade stand so your waiting customers have access to all the following information: Your business name and/or logo should be prominent so that the public can see who the artiste is. Within this should be a contact telephone number and a website address if you have one. Next to this should be the price that you are charging which is clear and not misleading. So if you decide to charge a higher price for working on adults than children, and the age difference, this should be shown. You will also need to have a health and safety disclaimer so that the customers are advised of the conditions that you will paint in/on and those that you won't (more on that in the health and safety chapter coming soon) and possibly any sort of self-promotion such as what you can be booked for, i.e. parties, fetes, fundays, etc. After this information will be your display menu to show off your face painting creations that you're offering at the event.

Display boards can be easily made by using 1 or 2 pieces of ply-wood that can be purchased from your local DIY store. These will need to be cut to your desired height and then painted in a colour of your choice which should be consistent to your branding. If you opt for using 2 pieces of board as you may have a lot of designs that you can offer then the two can be joined together to open out like a book by drilling some holes down one side of each piece and tying together with shoe-laces. These types of display boards can look tatty after a season so it's a good idea to refresh with a coat of paint in the winter ready again for the next summer. Your face painting display board needs to be kept as clean as possible so a good wiping down before each event will go a long way to keeping it looking nice and pristine. You'll be amazed at just how mucky it can get as the children like to touch and point at the faces using fingers that are covered in candy-floss or ice-cream. Oh yeah, and then there's those little darlings that like to kick the display board to indicate which face they'd like (not to mention one little boy who decided to have a wee against my display board)!!!!

If budget allows you may wish to purchase the free-standing display boards used for exhibition purposes. These are quite lightweight as they are generally made from aluminium and come in a range of colours for the cloth backing. The large roll-up promotional banners are another good way to display your designs however once you've had it printed and made the faces you have on it aren't interchangeable.

In the beginning you may have little or no professional photographic evidence that may be good enough for you to use for promotional purposes. The easiest way to display what you can offer is to simply have a design board that states the names of the faces that you can paint, such as Butterfly or Spiderman. This way your customers can choose what they would like to be painted as from your list of design names, which you can add to over time as your experience and confidence grows.

This will also help you as your customer is not choosing from a photograph that you will need to copy exactly, and you will have creative artistic licence to paint any type of Fairy or Monster that YOU so desire without them complaining that it doesn't look like the one in the photo! Often new face painters will take books along with them for their customers to choose a face from – this is a big mistake as some of the faces in the book they will be unable to paint and some they will not want to paint. Leave books at home and only use them for inspiration purposes.

The other good thing about having your display board showing design names only is that you'll be able to work with another face painter and work from the same display board. Your tiger may be completely different from the other painter's tiger, but it's your interpretation of a tiger. This way you both don't have to be painting exactly the same thing.

Under the copyright law you are not permitted to use other peoples' photographs that you have copied and pasted from search engines such as Google Images. Although a great source of inspiration for you to use, you cannot take other face painters creations, mount them on a display board, and offer the design to the public as yours. This work is copyrighted and not in your hand. Saying that, you can however copy the design by painting it onto your own model/child and then you can use that image for promotional purposes, as the art-work then becomes yours especially if you tweak it slightly and put your own touch to it. You also need to be careful under the copyright law of using names and words, such as Hello Kitty and Mickey Mouse for your design names as again this is copy-written to the originator as are football logos. Painting illegal, vulgar and offensive words are also heavily discouraged in our face painting industry.

If you're in the process of just starting your face painting business this can sometimes leave you very pushed for time especially if you have other paid employment. Essential tasks such as designing an impressive design board with your face painting designs on it that you'd like to offer your customers at events can be quite a daunting prospect and sometimes gets put on the back-burner. With this in mind, Mimicks is able to offer you a selection of laminated Design Cards and Price Cards to be used for your display purposes along with Copyright Free Face Painting Photographs which will present a professional and consistent image for you to use immediately. These can be found by visiting www.facepainting.uk.com

Event Equipment

Depending on the type of event that you're attending will determine how much equipment you'll need to take with you. From the children's birthday party where a kit-box and display board is generally all that you'll need right through to an event that you will be staying away overnight at is discussed next.

We're going to start with the easiest of all the events first:

➢ **Parties in people's homes** –
Your face painting kit which will include face paints, water cups, glitter, gemstones and glue, brushes stored in a pencil case or brush caddy, sponges stored in a plastic container, water dispenser or spritzer for dampening sponges, cotton-pads, surgical spirit, disposable brushes or cotton-buds, baby wipes, tablecloth, towel, overall or make-up cape and a mirror. All packed nicely in a kit box or roll-along case. You'll also need a display board, leaflets, promotional stickers, business cards and diary for any future enquiries.

➢ **Corporate Events**
All of the above.
Water carrier, empty water carrier for used water.
Table and either 2 chairs or a high chair.
Plastic covering in case it rains.
Promotional banner (optional).

➢ **School Fetes, Village Fetes and Community Fun Days**
All of the above.
Gazebo or trade stand, pegs for pinning stall down into grass, hammer, concrete blocks for pinning down on hard-standing areas, Face Painting signage.
Money bag, float, plastic bank bags.

➢ **Large Shows and Festivals**
All of the above, plus additional items for topping up such as more baby wipes, paints, etc.
Additional signage, ropes, grippers.
Additional tables and chairs,
Odds box containing safety pins, marker pens, pens, calculator, receipt pad, blu-tac and any other bits and bobs that you might need while you're there.
Overnight bag if you're staying away and tent and equipment if you intend to camp.

The lists above of course are not inclusive of everything that you may need as each face painter has different requirements. It's always a good idea to have a typed out resource list that you can check off for all the types of events that you'll be doing so as you pack the things that you will be needing you can make a quick double-check from your list to check you've got everything.

I had an annoying situation once when we were 1½ hours into our travelling time heading for a show up North when I suddenly realised I'd left all the brushes at home for me and my staff to use. My poor hubby had to drop us all off at a service station then belt back home to pick up the brushes and then drive back to us, and then drive onwards to the show. Another time I forgot all my sponges and had to use a cut up kitchen cloth (a new one I hasten to add) to apply the base work, and on yet another occasion I left a whole storage box with 6 face painting kits in it at home. Not good!

CHAPTER 9

Putting Systems
In Place

Business Administration

Maybe by now you have done a couple of parties, a village community event here and there and a few corporate paid events and are now looking towards getting a system together regarding your paperwork. To run a business effectively, a dependable business administration system needs to be put in place. For without some kind of structure to not only your face painting bookings and events but also your administration, you could easily find yourself becoming overwhelmed with it all and on the other hand becoming despondent and losing the passion that you once had when starting out.

It can be very easy to tie yourself up completely in the running of your business by sacrificing your health, family and sanity. In order for you to own the business and for it not to own you, you will need to develop effective systems that will deliver foreseeable results from routine use. A business system is relatively easy to put into place from start-up as it will be a step by step process, and each building block that you put in place will form a structure in which to build the next block from.

When all businesses start out they start from nothing apart from the first seedling, the first idea. Over time as the business grows so does the ideas regarding the systems on how the business will operate which have been tried and tested through trial and error. The big National branded companies were also once there right at the beginning as a start-up company, like we all were, and have spent many years perfecting their business format. They too once went out and purchased their first batch of business cards, designed their first letterhead and put together a basic brochure in which to woo and attract their clients or customers. You will be doing the same as they did.

All your paper-based sales material should be consistent in image, which includes colour, typeface and logo, if you have one. People can become easily confused about your image if it's all over the place with one style of writing for this, a different colour for that and varying styles of a logo. Think long and hard about your image and how you wish to portray your business and reflect your style, and keep it consistent in all areas at all times. Before you rush off out there to have any of your sales material printed, it's a good idea to have a friend proof read your item in case of any typos or grammar issues that may be flagged up.

So to start with the real basics of a good administration system, which will include your sales material, let's start with the simplest of all humble essentials:

Business Cards

This is without a doubt one of the first investments you need to make just at the onset of your face painting venture. No matter how large or small you anticipate your growth within the industry, your business card will be an essential element for your future growth.

You will encounter many opportunities to hand your card to prospective customers, to use as a referral or to take with you when meeting suppliers or networking. Without one in your purse, wallet or handbag is an admission that you are not as serious as you thought you were about your business and that lack of passion will be felt by others. 'Hey, can I have your business card' – 'Ooops sorry, haven't got one on me'. Oh dear!

If you are designing your own business card you will find that print-shops on the Internet will display the image sizes, format and resolution that you can follow to produce your own. Some even provide templates for you to use – but these can be pretty basic. You may be lucky enough to know someone in graphic design who will be happy for you to commission them for your project.

After you're business card has been designed and is ready to go to print you can again search the web where you'll find an abundant of printers listed on the Internet that you can choose from, quotes tend to be instant as well, and prices range from free to very cheap to very expensive. A word of warning here though – do be wary of the free type as these sometimes require that you have the name of the print company printed on the reverse of your card. This can de-value your business and you could be considered a cheap-skate for choosing freebies which will reflect on the quality of the service that you provide.

In the beginning its best not to order a run of too many cards as over the first couple of months of handing them out to prospective customers you are bound to find things that you are not quite happy with, and you will want to make changes for improvement, which you can do prior to the next run of them. Small print runs of say fifty are a good start.

On receipt of you business card, be sure to always have a small batch about your person, in your kit box or in your car. You never ever know when an opportunity will present itself, and there's nothing worse than promoting yourself to someone, then rummaging around in your handbag, and not having something tangible to give to the other person to remember you by! I always make a point of sending a business card out with my confirmation of bookings, invoices and just generally any letter I send out in the post. People are likely to keep a business card that has been sent to them as it's easy for them to pop it into their purse, wallet or business card holder – and hey presto it's easily retrievable should the moment arise that they are able to recommend you. Don't miss a trick for promotion.

Letterheads

With your business card now in place, it's time to create your letterhead. This will have the same branding image as above and again only a small quantity will need to be purchased in the beginning.

Your letterhead will be used for mailing out to customers with details of any up and coming promotions, event quotations, additional services offered and any personal correspondence you may wish to send out. Incidentally you should always make an effort to find out the name of the person that you're contacting, especially in a business capacity as no-one likes to receive a letter headed 'Dear Sir/Madam' or at worst 'To Whom it May Concern'! Get personal and get noticed.

You will also use your letterhead to contact trade suppliers and to contact your bank, your accountant, the Inland Revenue and possibly your local Council. A letterhead creates a professional image and can also double up as the document you use to print appointment reminders, invoices, receipts and confirmation of bookings. This is especially beneficial for your accounts that are invoiced after the actual event booking takes place.

Even a small run of a hundred will be worthwhile in the beginning, but don't forget that you will pay a more premium price for small quantities. If you're designing and printing your own letterheads you can give them a more professional feel to them by using a top quality paper like Conqueror.

Leaflets

Your leaflet needs to give a *brief* outline of the type of face painting service that you offer, a sort of taster or menu if you like, from which the customer can become interested to find out more about. The leaflet, whether single-sided or double-sided doesn't need to go into specific detail, but just enough information to whet the customers appetite, enough for them to seek you out further and even look at you website for a comprehensive account of what you do, if you have one.

Leaflets are similar to business cards but bigger and with additional information, and should be used in the same way – ready to be produced to a prospective customer in any given moment. They are also a good tool for mail-shots, or to leave on counters at complimentary businesses (children's clothes shops as an example) or to place as a loose leaf inside the local community directory or newspaper.

Your leaflets can change their appearance as often as you see fit, maybe when you launch a new service to promote a holiday theme like Halloween or Christmas. It is also quite usual to have a couple of different styles of leaflets going at the same time.

Less is more as far as your leaflet is concerned, so try not to over-cram it with too much information, ridiculously small print and irrelevant particulars. Don't be afraid of 'white space' as this can give the impression of calmness and clarity to what you are offering – however too much white space can also be a wasted opportunity for your business promotion! So get the balance right.

Brochures

The business brochure is probably one of the hardest and most complicated of all the sales material to produce. Your brochure can make or break you and can speak volumes about your business and the class of service that you provide.

The first consideration you will need to take is what size and style to produce it in and this can be tricky as there is so much to choose from. Styles come in all shapes and sizes from single-fold to bi-fold, from tri-fold to gate-fold, and from A4, A5 and A6 multi-page brochures in a landscape or portrait manner. Phew – such a choice!

Once you've decided on your budget and on the style of brochure the next job is to think about what you would like to include in it. Just write a brainstormed list to start with (or have yourself a blue-sky moment as they say now)! Next make a draft copy of the brochure size and its layout, being sure to put the creases in the correct place if you intend on having a folded one.

Then, in pencil, start transferring the information from your list onto the draft copy positioning each item as you see fit. If you have many services to promote it's best to place them into similar groups for easier reading as you want your prospective customer to feel comfortable with the layout and not have to search for crucial information as their reading experience will need to flow. At this stage it's important to place your business name and logo in a prominent position, and all the contact information necessary as you don't want to have to squeeze this in as an after-thought.

If you are adept at using a graphics editor such as Photoshop or Fireworks you may wish to also plan it out there as you can easily build layers which you can drag and drop into their relevant place. Printing your draft copy out will also give you a greater understanding of how your finished item will look.

Areas to take into consideration, when planning out your brochure, is firstly the layout as above, and secondly the text (copy) that you will be adding. Do you want to provide comprehensive explanations on each of your services or just bulleted lists with a brief description? Either way, make sure that it relates the benefits to the customer, which is discussed in detail in my book 'Growing Your Profitable Face Painting Business', which is the result of the service that you'll provide.

A bad example of not outlining the benefits would be:
Face Painting Parties – all areas covered by an established professional face painter.

A good example of outlining the benefits would be:
Face Painting at Your Son or Daughter's Birthday Party – a fantastic and fun activity for all, regardless of their age. We'll keep your guests fully entertained providing you with valuable time to chat with the parents as we transform the

girls into butterflies, princesses and fairies and the boys into monsters, tigers and super-heroes.

All of the copy used throughout your brochure should be customer focused by using the words 'You' and 'Your' to communicate the benefits of the service and what it will do for them. This makes it more personal to them and as they read it will make them feel that's it's all been written about them for them. Great psychology at its best! This is not the place for your own ego boost on how professional you are, how brilliant your face painting is or how many years you've been established. The brochure is all about the customer and what they want, need or desire, not you.

Before you have a complete run of brochures printed, it is advisable to see a sample copy prior to placing a confirmed order as this could bring to light any spelling or grammar mistakes, any misalignment of text or images and any colour considerations that may need to be altered. It's imperative that you do use a spell checker and also a high resolution for any photographs used, as your print-shop will unlikely check these things out for you and may not be held accountable.

You will be exited and apprehensive for your first batch to arrive, and when it does, then proudly hand them out to anyone and everyone for maximum exposure!

Complimentary Slips

A complimentary slip is not a necessity; however it's a nice thing to have. Based upon similar styles to your letterhead, you can use your complimentary slip to send hand-written notes to customers or suppliers, and also use as a packing slip if sending products or freebies out in the post.

Invoices

Nothing looks more professional than a quality formatted invoice. These days it is not necessary to purchase expensive invoice pads that have been custom designed by your print-shop, as you can quite easily prepare and produce invoices from your own computer and colour printer.

Your invoice will need to have all your company details printed on at the top, which will include business name and address, telephone and mobile number, email address and website. You'll also need to include a company registration number if you are a Limited company and a VAT number if you are VAT registered. Incidentally – VAT registration is only applicable when your turnover reaches a certain level. Your invoices need to be numbered in sequential order from the very first time you issue one and this numbering system must be consistent throughout your business life.

As an invoice is a request for payment from a client, customer or supplier, etc, it should also indicate somewhere about your preferred payment methods. If accepting cheques then the name in which the cheque is to be made payable too needs to be clearly shown, and if you accept BACS payments then the details of your business bank account must also be provided – sort code and account number. Incidentally you'll need a business bank account to run a business. Using a personal account to pay cheques into from your customers will lose credibility.

An invoice can either be just a typed-out document outlining the services or products rendered or it can be produced in a table format which will enable you to list multiple items. You don't even have to start from scratch when designing your invoice as there are plenty of templates to be found on the Internet.

When printing out your invoice it is essential to also print a duplicate copy that you will need to keep for your book-keeping records which you'll be handling over to your accountant. If you intend to have accounts with corporate bookers whereby they can pay on terms (14, 21, 30 days, etc) then it will be necessary to send them an invoice outlining the service particulars and costs. Your duplicate copy that you will keep on file will serve as a reminder to you regarding outstanding debts that are owed.

Receipts

On collecting a cash or cheque payment from a customer on the day a service has been completed, you can use a receipt pad for this purpose. It is not necessary to print your own pads as these little booklets can be purchased from most good stationery shops. They are quite self-explanatory and all that needs to be documented is the date, the customer's name (and possibly address), the service provided and the fee paid to you.

Again the receipt pad will need to be in a numbered order and the duplicate copy must be kept for your records. Pads usually come in duplicate sheets of a hundred and for your records you can prefix the batch of numbers with A, B, C, etc. For example A1 through to A100, and the next receipt pad purchased would be B1 through to B100, and so on and so on. This will assign a specific 'folio' number for each pad that you purchase that will be easily recognisable to you and your accountant when organising your book-keeping for that financial year.

Your Bookings Diary

Your bookings diary is the lifeline of all your business activities and should be easily retrievable at a moment's notice. There is nothing worse than having a prospective customer on the phone wishing to make a booking and all of a sudden your diary has gone 'walkies'. Over the years I have used many different styles and types of booking-in systems and have gone from large day-per-page diaries to those little miniscule pocket ones (which I must add were an absolute waste of time).

I find that the 'week at a glance' is by far the best choice, as when an enquiry comes in I can open the diary at the relevant week and can see immediately what my availability is. I use different coloured pens to book in different types of bookings or commitments, and in pencil I include any provisional arrangements that have also been made or quoted on. Never miss an opportunity for future business – take your bookings diary with you to all events as you never know who is going to ask if you're available on a particular date.

As well as my bookings diary I also keep a ring-binder folder with monthly section dividers in it, and in there I place any information for services being provided for each specific month or to store details of other bookings or commitments that are coming up. By keeping a folder of this kind organises all the monthly paperwork, booking forms and other documents which can be easily retrieved without having to search through a messy in-tray. This ring-binder also serves as a back-up for the diary.

So with the few business basics as listed above the next step is to write a handy script to follow for when your prospective customer phones to make an enquiry.

Pre Written Scripts

If you are new to business it can be quite a daunting prospect when the phone rings and your intuition says that it's an enquiry from a customer. By having a pre-written script close to the phone you need never have to worry about what to say to the person on the other end of the line.

In order to write a script it is necessary to go through the process of role-play, whereby you are the customer and you are also yourself. Take a sheet of paper and start to brainstorm a conversation on how the enquiry might go.

Start off by scripting how you would like to answer the phone call. Remember that you are in business and it can be quite off-putting if you just pick-up and say 'Hello'. Speaking out loud to yourself, try saying "Hello [and your name] speaking", or perhaps try saying "Hello [and your business name]". This time say "Good Morning, [your name], how can I help you". Now try the above again but this time say it with a big smile, it will almost always sound different coming from a cheery disposition.

Next, the prospective client will usually say "Oh Hi, yeah I'm just phoning up about ....." and she will speak a sentence or so either about her requirements or about an advert she's seen, or for the further information outlined in your brochure. Listen with care at this point, don't interrupt and only speak when she has stopped talking. If she gives you her name, make a point of writing it down immediately and you can then use it during the conversation with her and she will be most impressed that you have remembered it.

Your next job is to confidently answer her query with as much information as possible. During this stage you should ask her open-ended questions in order to gain more information on her requirements. Each time the prospective customer speaks; you must stop talking and listen to what he or she has to say. Their part of the conversation is the most important aspect so try to avoid butting in inappropriately. This, however, can sometimes be difficult to do as we just want to provide the customer with as much information about our business as possible as our passion for our industry takes over.

After you have given the customer the necessary details which might also include the price, it is time to close the sale and make the booking. During the phone call you would have located your diary and be in a position to offer her the date and time. Not all enquiries however will turn to a committed booking and if you feel that you are losing her or she states that she'd like to go away and think about it (or the usual one whereby she says she needs to check with her husband first) ask if you can take her email address so that you can forward her a quotation outlining the details of the service she has enquired about and offer to send her your special report/newsletter. By offering her something free and something of value should make a good impression about who you are and what your business is all about. This customer will now be intrigued, so act upon sending her this free information as soon as you can, preferably within a couple of hours.

Should your customer make a booking with you, this part of the script will include taking details of the service required, her full name and address, and the address where the event is taking place. It is also important to take a contact telephone number and I always make a point of taking both a land-line and a mobile number and of course an email address.

Thank her very much for her booking and let her know that you look forward to meeting her soon. Also let her know that you will send out the confirmation details in the post. Customers like to have hard-copies of the booking as it makes it more official and definite. This pre-written script will be the format to follow for all enquiries regardless of the service required.

Other scripts that you might like to write are for telephoning your customers about promotions and special offers, or new service launches.

Information Forms

The most used types of information forms that you'll need are booking forms and customer enquiry forms.

When that 'oh so important' customer enquiry comes in by phone there is nothing worse than reaching out for a piece of paper to write down the event details on when all you can lay your hand to is a scrappy piece of paper, the corner of a local newspaper or your child's beautiful colouring picture. This is not good business practice. You need a pre-formatted information forms ready to hand - and you also need a batch of pens as well, you know the ones I mean - the type that write!

My hubby is guilty of this offence quite often, and I feel exasperated when I find that my tidy 'to do lists' or 'notes to self' have random telephone numbers, people's names and dates written on them in the corner – without explanation. Does this slapdash scribbling mean anything to me, not in the least, does it mean anything to him, he can't remember!

A booking form will capture all the hand-written details necessary to transfer over to a typed confirmation of booking form and then into your bookings diary. For an enquiry without a booking being made you'll need an enquiry form.

Your Booking Form will need to record the following details:

- Customers Name
- Address
- Telephone Number
- Mobile Number
- Email Address
- Date and time of event
- Type of event
- Any special requirements
- Are they providing shelter, table and chairs, water
- How did they hear about you
- Were they referred and if so by whom

Information forms can be designed quite simply on your computer, and I usually do two to a page, cut them through and secure each pad with a bulldog clip. Your enquiry form can be based on similar information that you'll need to gather. Again these pads are kept by the telephone for immediate use. With information sheets like this to hand will make for a very efficient business administration system.

Dealing With Customer Paperwork

For well over two decades Mimicks Face Painting has been using the same system with regards to customer paperwork. Obviously it has changed quite dramatically in appearance over the years as in the early 1990's a typewriter was used instead of a computer - oh how old fashioned!

It will be necessary for you to send your customers that book your service, whether a private party booker or a corporate booker, a confirmation of booking that summarizes all the particulars of their event. This will outline the customers address, venue address, telephone numbers, email address, date and time of event, service being provided and the cost. You will need to print a duplicate copy for yourself that you can keep in your bookings folder under the relevant month which can be retrieved when you need it.

As well as sending them a confirmation of booking you should also include a document that has your terms and conditions on and a copy for them to sign in agreement and return back to you with their deposit cheque, or confirmation of their bank transfer.

After the event has taken place, preferably the next working day, you will send your corporate bookers an invoice for services rendered, stating your payment terms. An example of all three of these forms can be found at the back of this book.

Once you have designed your own documents you will save them as a file in a folder on your computer and every time you need to send out a confirmation or invoice it will be easy for you to open the document, change the details to the current customer and post out to them. Do take care, however, in making sure that you change all the particulars necessary as I once sent out an invoice to a customer for a £95 booking fee but the invoice total showed £1875. They were a bit confused to say the least. I've also made the mistake a few times whereby I've forgot to change the customer's name and have sent out a conformation for a party in the wrong name!

Storing Your Business Records

With your bookshelf at the ready that we discussed in an earlier chapter you will now need to fill it with files and folders of all sorts and if you're anything like me, I have to have all my files of sort in a particular colour and style (OCD or what)!

Below is a list of all the types of files and folders that I have at the ready to place the relevant paperwork into:

- Customer Bookings Folder
  Information forms, consultation sheets, confirmation of bookings (past) address, email and telephone databases. Data protection could apply here so contact the Information Commissioners Office (ICO). In here I also keep internet release forms and allergy declaration forms.

- Invoice Folder
  Invoices awaiting payment and invoices paid

- Training Folder
  Any information regarding forthcoming courses that you'd like to attend to enhance your skills, new product launches that you may wish to invest in and details of forthcoming trade shows and maybe a list of all business books you'd like to read.

- Products Folder
  Current information about the products that you use including ingredient lists, wholesale price-lists and suppliers details, along with website information for other product suppliers.

- Health and Safety Folder
  To store all information related to health and safety, codes of practice, risk assessments, method statements, insurances, local bye-law information, affiliations and trade memberships.

- Swipe Files
  For absolutely anything that you have taken from other sources that you can use for inspiration in your advert writing, brochure design layouts, business colour schemes, ideas, tips and tricks. As the name implies – it's something that you have swiped from somewhere else to help you at a later date and could include photographs, images, wordings for copy-writing and even your competitor's leaflets, etc.

The next batch of folders contains information that I fully discuss in my other book, but its well worth you having these folders at the ready:

- Book Keeping Folder(s)
  This can be quite extensive as you will need income folders and outgoings folders, along with bank statements, etc.

- Action Planning Folder(s)
  All your lists for daily to do's, weekly to do's and monthly to do's, time management plans and self analysis forecasts.

- Customer Records Folder
  Anything and everything to do with your target market and who your customer is, customer surveys and testimonials.

- Business Planning Folder
  For your objective master plans, cash-flow plans and finance plans.

As well as the customary files and folders kept on your book-shelf you will also need to allocate a specific folder on your computer or laptop solely for your business venture. This folder can then be split into many individual folders to store documents such as invoices, confirmations, scripts, information forms, emails to send, databases and adverts, etc. As well as keeping this type of information stored on your computer you should also save it to a memory stick or external hard-drive as a back-up and it's also worth printing out hard-copies of all of these documents as well and then storing this information in a folder named General Admin.

Systems deliver expected and reliable results. Systems will give you more control over your business, better management of your time, less pressure and a better relationship with your customers. Always make every effort to put a system in place, no matter how small or insignificant it may seem, as they can absolutely transform your business and your working practices. Don't let your business own you – you need to take control and own it.

CHAPTER 10

Legal Requirements

The Inland Revenue

Being self-employed and running your own face painting business is not as hard as you may think with regards to keeping on the right side of the law and keeping up with the paperwork – as long as you put systems in place from the onset which will be briefly explained in this chapter. I would, however, also seek to take further advice from an accountant or other business advisor as there are additional requirements that you will need to be aware of when running a small business. So what are the basic requirements that you need to follow? Written here is just a brief explanation of what is needed to get you going and to keep you on the right side of the law.

As soon as you set up in business for yourself it's a good idea to notify the Inland Revenue as soon as possible, regardless as to whether you have made your first sale or not.

By doing so they will have all the information needed about you and your business venture for when the times comes that you start taking money from a paid service from a friend or customer. The moment cash, cheque or card exchanges hand – that's the moment you're in business, no matter whether it's for a fiver from your best friend or for a tenner from the lady down the road. You're in business. If you delay registering, you may have to pay an initial penalty fee. You'll also have to pay further penalties if payments of tax become due and have not yet been met.

When you become self-employed you must register for Income Tax and National Insurance purposes with HM Revenue & Customs. If you are in a partnership, each of the partners must also register separately.

The information that they require will be:

- Name
- Address
- National Insurance Number
- Date of Birth
- Telephone Number
- Email address
- Date Self-Employment Commenced
- Nature of Your Business
- Business Address – if different from above
- Business Telephone Number – if different from above
- The Business's Unique Tax Reference if you are joining an existing partnership and the business partners details

Make sure you have all of this information to hand if registering online as you can't save the details and return at a later date once you have started to complete the online form. You will then be issued with your very own UTR code (Unique Tax Reference) which you'll use for all your self-employed dealings throughout your business life.

You won't need to register for VAT until your taxable turnover reaches a certain limit, and there's plenty of advice available when it does from the Inland Revenue website. HMRC also provides free workshops and events that help new and expanding businesses progress through tax and VAT requirements.

For further information regarding self-employment, income tax and national insurance contributions, visit their website at www.hmrc.gov.uk

Basic Book Keeping

Being self-employed requires you to keep a record of accounts which isn't half as scary as you may think, as all it takes in the beginning is a couple of spreadsheets that you can easily format in Excel, or as a table format in MS Word. Think of your book keeping as having two baskets – one which you will fill with all records of money going out, and the other you will fill with all records of money coming in (which hopefully should be the bigger one of the two)!

Let's now make a list of everything you're going to put into basket number one, the things going out:

Expenses – also known as Business Outgoings

Expenditure receipts are items that you have spent money on to run your business and can include things such as:

- Product supplies – all materials needed to provide your services.
- Tools and equipment – items purchased to enhance the application of your services.
- Rents and commissions – fees paid to attend any events such as shows, festivals and fetes.
- Reference books and magazines to keep you up-to-date with current industry trends.
- Uniform that you have purchased to keep within the professional standards of the industry.
- Stationary and sundry items purchased to help put business administration systems in place.
- Printing costs – all the materials needed for your sales literature and the promotion of your business such as brochures and business cards.
- Advertising – placed in magazines, newspapers and the like.
- Online advertising which will include your domain purchase, website costs, hosting package and any Adwords campaigns.
- Office equipment such as computer, printer, software, desk, chair and bookcase.
- Postage spent on stamps for communication to your clients and suppliers and courier charges for sending out packages.
- Professional fees to your accountant, business advisor and for any professional training courses undertaken.
- Motor expenses – this would include repair costs and road tax and the fuel and oil that are needed to run your car on a

daily basis to get to and from your events, suppliers, etc. Log book, valuation, emission, and purchase record regarding the vehicle must also be kept.

- Telephone – a proportion of the bill from your land-line and mobile phone will be tax deductible, so keep the complete invoice and your accountant will be able to apportion it for you based on usage.

- Overheads – this will include any additional council tax or business rates that you pay on your home as a business premise.

- Insurance and licenses – your public liability and product liability premiums as well as any charges made from your local council regarding trading bye-laws.

- Repairs and servicing of any of your face painting equipment including electrical PAT testing.

- Equipment hire – this could include things such as compressors, gas cylinders or fire extinguishers.

- Drawings made by you from the business bank for your personal wages and expenses.

- Bank charges that your bank will produce from your business account and any credit card fees if you have a card payment facility set up. This also includes any PayPal or Google Checkout transaction fees.

- Rental and rates overheads if you have business premises or a shop.

Your expense records will come from your bank statements, your company cheque book and any credit card statements. All cash expenses must also be recorded by documenting small purchase receipts.

As you can see it is quite a comprehensive list. If in doubt of what receipts and sales invoices to keep – then keep them all and your accountant will be able to advise you accordingly at the end of your financial year. Oh incidentally – your financial year runs from the date that you started and registered your business and doesn't necessarily mean from January through to December as it could very well be from September 23rd through to September 22nd the following year, or whatever time you notified the Inland Revenue of your business start-up.

Income – also known as 'Money in the Bank'
Your business income will come from sources such as:

- Services provided
- Products sold for retail purposes
- Any training provision that you are in a position to give to others for a fee being paid
- Any pieces of equipment used in the business that you sell on as second-hand
- Any other miscellaneous income that is linked to the business
- Interest paid to your business bank account by your bank

Your income records will come from your invoices that you raise to your customers and from the receipt books that you keep. Other records of income are your bank statements and your paying-in book. All income in cash payments must also be documented.

Record Keeping

As well as your cheque book, paying-in book, bank and credit card statements you should also keep records of petty cash spent, an inventory of stock and working products in hand, a list of capital equipment that you have purchased and any details of money taken out from the account for your own personal and private use, along with details of any personal money invested into the business.

Organising Your Accounts

Basically – three lever-arch folders with dividers is all that you will need.

EXPENSES FOLDER:

In your first lever-arch folder, place into it 12 monthly section dividers. Under each month you will file all the invoices and receipts that you have collected from basket one, in descending date order for the month. At the beginning of each month, place in a plastic wallet and in here you can store all the little petty cash receipts that you're unable to hole-punch.

On the receipts and invoices that you are storing in here, write in red pen across the top of the bill how much the invoice was for and whether it was paid by cash, cheque or card. If it was paid by cheque you will also need to write the cheque number here as well.

File information in this folder on a daily basis as a discipline if you can or at least weekly and keep this system going for each month. This makes up your expenses folder. If done on a regular basis it will grow easily and you won't need to spend countless hours trying to sort it all out at the end of your financial year.

INCOME FOLDER:

Your second lever-arch folder will be organised on the same principle as the first, with similar 12 monthly dividers, however this time it will contain the invoices and receipts from income earned through services rendered and products sold. Again, file the information in this folder on a regular basis and keep this system going for each month. This makes up your income folder.

ACCOUNTS FOLDER:

In your third lever-arch file, place in 5 section dividers and label then with the following titles: Expenses, Income, Statements, Drawings (wages), and Miscellaneous documents.

In the Expenses section you will file the 12 spreadsheets for the year's expense accounts (more about these in a moment) and in the Income section you will file the spreadsheets for the year's income accounts.

Your bank statements will be stored in the next section and will include those from the bank, from your credit card company, from PayPal and any building society that you may hold. A drawings and wages spreadsheet will follow in the next section and in the last of the section dividers you can keep any additional miscellaneous information that your accountant may need, such as any P45's from other employment, any correspondence from the Inland Revenue, stock control sheets, equipment resource information and vehicle details. This makes up your accounts folder.

Account Spreadsheets

An Excel spreadsheet is the easiest way to record your accounts on your computer until you progress to using specific software for the task such as Sage Instant Accounts.

Make it a discipline to update your spreadsheets on a weekly basis by entering the information that you have stored in your Expenses folder and your Income folder, in order to keep on top of it all. If you fail to do this you may find it can become overwhelming if you have many entries to post and your memory doesn't serve you well in remembering all the necessary information. For an even more effective method you could even do it on a daily basis and that way it shouldn't take too long. As you reach the end of each month and all entries have been posted you can print off a copy to store in your Accounts folder. Always make a back-up on saving the changes on your computer so that you have a failsafe system in place.

At the end of your financial year and prior to the self-assessment deadline of January 31st – you can hand over your three very organised folders to your accountant for revision, and I'm sure he or she will be very impressed with the organisation of your paperwork.

Your accountant will use these records to create a profit and loss account for you, which will let you know how much income was generated and what expenses were paid out over the financial year, and whether you have made a profit or a loss. The more detailed records you keep, the easier it will be to answer any questions that your accountant or the Inland Revenue may have regarding your tax return.

Your business accounts need to be stored safely for five years after the normal filing deadline of 31st January and this will also include the safe storage of your appointment books and business diaries.

This business guide has been written for the UK market – please seek professional advice for other Countries on Legal Requirements.

CHAPTER 11

Hygiene Techniques and Procedures

Cross Infection Control

There are certain circumstances and situations where you will not be able to work on a particular child or adult for health and safety implications and customers must be able to trust their judgement knowing that the industry as a whole is ensuring the protection of them.

Face Painting without infection control can be a breeding ground for germs so your main concern is to consider how to maintain a state of cleanliness sufficient to prohibit the growth of bacterial and viral infections.

Transfer of infection can be by direct contact through:

- Touching an infected person by fingers, sponge or brush or the passing of germs when speaking, coughing or sneezing

Transfer of infection can be by indirect contact through:

- Using an infected sponge, brush or product which will pass on the infection from that object to the person

To avoid transfer of infection or cross-contamination you must strictly follow these basic guidelines:

- Wash your hands prior to any face painting activities
- Check your customer for any contra-indications that could either prevent or restrict the face painting application (see below)
- Do not work on anyone with an infection or skin disease
- Do not touch virulent infected areas on yourself. Ideally you should not work if you have a cold sore or have conjunctivitis
- Cover your open cuts and wounds with a suitable dressing
- Move away from your customer when coughing or blowing your nose and wash your hands immediately afterwards
- Cleanse hands as often as is practical during a face painting session with wipes and alcoholic gel
- Sterilise all equipment thoroughly before and after each session
- Never let waste accumulate on your work area - dispose of it immediately
- Don't re-use any items or equipment that have been dropped onto the floor such as brushes or sponges – wrap, take home and sterilise

- Keep your work area clean and tidy

Contra Indications that Prevent and Restrict

A contra-indication is a condition which is infectious or non-infectious that will prevent you from working on your customer or that will restrict the face painting application to a specific area. Always, always perform a visual inspection on your customer prior to the face painting taking place. Remember the word MENS for this purpose, checking thoroughly the Mouth, Eyes, Nose and Skin.

The following diseases, disorders and conditions will *prevent* any face painting activity taking place; therefore you will be unable to work on anyone with:

- Cold Sores
- Conjunctivitis
- Styes
- Impetigo
- Influenza
- Active Chicken Pox
- Severe Acne
- Open cuts and wounds and new bruising
- Sunburn and flaking skin
- Any known allergies
- Positive patch test result

The following disorders and conditions will *restrict* face painting in specific areas; therefore you must avoid the following immediate areas:

- Chicken Pox scabs
- Heavy Colds
- Eczema and Dermatitis
- Recent bruising
- Lanolin intolerance

Children who find it very hard to still and those with a nervous disposition will also restrict a face painting application and therefore contra-indicated. In this instance you could offer something smaller and quicker to apply like a little motif/tattoo on their arm or hand.

Any adults under the influence of alcohol or who are verbally abusive must also be refused.

Head-lice is a childhood condition that affects most families at one time or another, and it will be at your discretion as to whether a face painting application can go ahead. You will notice head-lice usually after sweeping the child's fringe away from their face and you may notice small silvery eggs clinging to the hair close to the root. If you do continue to paint, before moving onto the next customer you must cleanse your hands thoroughly with a wipe and then use an alcoholic gel. You will also need to quickly change your water and wipe over your brushes with surgical spirit. Remember that you are touching the heads of many people, which is a potential opportunity for head lice to reallocate from one head to another.

Adverse Skin Conditions

Generally an adverse skin condition like Vitiligo is safe to work on as it is not a disease or infection. However it is good practice to ask the customer if there is any discomfort within the area so you will be able to adapt the pressure of painting accordingly. If in doubt as to what a suspected condition is you can always diplomatically ask the customer.

Contra Actions

A contra-action is a reaction to a product that has been applied almost immediately or over a period of time. There are two types of contra actions that may take place after the face painting has been applied, and both give no rise to concern. The usual feeling post-painting is that of:

- Tightness to the skin. This is caused by the water evaporating from the product leaving a layer of make-up pigment left on the skins surface

- Ticklish feeling to the skin. This is caused by the hairs on the skin springing back up to their natural alignment after the water has evaporated

The contra-actions giving rise for concern post-painting is that of:

- Erythema (reddening of the skin)

- Blistering and hives of any kind
- Excessive stinging or burning
- Feeling sick or being sick
- Generally feeling unwell

Should the customer experience any of the above then it is probable that they are having an allergic reaction to the products applied. Depending on the severity of the reaction the face painting product must be removed immediately. In very rare cases the customer should be taken to hospital immediately for advice or treatment and you will need to have full product ingredients to hand along with the actual pots of paint that may have caused the reaction.

It is recommended that you keep a full product information and ingredient list in your kit as a printed document should it be needed for customer viewing or to be used during an emergency.

Allergies and Known Irritants Patch Tests

People with skin disorders such as eczema or dermatitis (mild or severe) or those that have had *any* known allergies should have a patch test done in advance of any face painting application.

If you do decide to paint someone with the above conditions or those that have told you of a previous reaction then you must, must, must perform a patch test to the products and colours you will be using. To do this you will need to paint on small stripes of the intended colours onto the customers inside wrist or onto the crook of the elbow and ask them to leave it on for about thirty minutes. Unlike the beauty industry whereby we administer a 24-48 hour patch test on certain products it is not possible to do this at a short time-span event like a school-fete. When they return to you after thirty minutes if no reaction is noted then face painting could commence *but only at the utmost risk of the customer*. You will need to fully explain that you cannot be held responsible should a reaction occur on the face even though no reaction has appeared on the patch test area. If they have informed you of a previous reaction to any type of face painting products of any kind I would strongly advise that you REFUSE application. Your insurance policy will more than likely not stand up in court if you were told of any previous reactions by the customer. Under no circumstances guide the customer or even influence them in any way at all by making statements that your products are perfectly safe, apart from warning them that it is still possible that a skin reaction could occur. In this situation you will need the customer to sign an Allergy Declaration form to safeguard your working practices and to assist you should a claim arise against you; however this may not give you the protection you will need in court.

When face painting at children's birthday parties you will need to ask the party parent to inform all the parents of the kiddies attending that face painting will be taking place. This way any child who has had a previous reaction, or has any known allergies or who is unsuitable for face painting for whatever reason, then their parent will be able to inform the party Mum that he/she is not allowed to take part in that activity.

See sample Allergy Declaration Form at the back of the book.

Health and Safety Disclaimer

Your face painting display board must have a Health and Safety Disclaimer clearly displayed and visible for all queuing customers to read.

This disclaimer will inform customers of the conditions that will prevent the face painting application taking place such as a list of all contra-indications and known allergies, along with being unable to work on children who find it hard to sit still or who become distressed during the application.

Face painting health and safety disclaimers are available to purchase as a laminated sign from www.facepainting.uk.com

CHAPTER 12

Following Legislation And Standards

Safe Working Practices

Although face painting can be deemed as something that 'anyone can do' as products are widely sold on the general consumer market, there is a certain amount of skill in application that is necessary along with the knowledge of trading implications that are required not only by law but also as common practice to ensure the safety and wellbeing of our customers – both adults and children alike. Your workplace requirements will need to reflect the standards of the beauty industry as a whole taking into consideration hygiene implications, cleanliness along with maintaining all health and safety implications.

The law demands that every place of employment is a healthy and safe place to work in, for the employer, the employees and the customers/clients. Failure to comply can have serious consequences and may result in claims for damages and injuries, loss of trade through bad publicity and even closure of trading.

The following chapter briefly outlines all the units that I cover when teaching the VTCT make-up qualifications at college and I think that to be a face painter in this ever expanding industry you should never become complacent about having enough background knowledge relating to legislation and health and safety.

Health and Safety at Work Act

The Health and Safety at Work Act provides a legal framework to encourage health and safety standards in the workplace. This basically means that when running your face painting events you must ensure that your working practices conform to safe standards and that your working environment is safe for the public to enter into. Regardless as to whether you're an employer or an employee you will both have responsibilities under this Act.

The employer of the face painting business must:

- Safeguard the health and safety of themselves, their employees and members of the public
- Keep all products and equipment being used up to a good standard and ensure that it is fit for the intended purpose, i.e., the correct type of brush used for the face painting activity and fully regulated products
- Provide safety measures to be taken which are recorded in the companies face painting risk assessments, ensuring that safe systems of work are in place for all concerned

- Have all electrical equipment checked regularly where necessary which includes having current PAT testing certificates
- Ensure the environment is free from toxic fumes
- Ensure that all staff are aware of all safety procedures to be followed as good practice especially when working on children, and by providing up to date product and equipment training where necessary for them

The employee must:

- Take reasonable care to avoid injury to themselves, to their customers, to colleagues and to others
- Co-operate effectively and competently with their employer, colleagues and customer
- Not to interfere or misuse anything that has been provided to protect their health and safety

Fire Precaution

In the event of a fire in the workplace it is your priority to remove customers and yourself to safety as quickly as possible.

This Act enforces that:

- All premises have fire-fighting equipment, so it is likely that you'll need to provide suitable extinguishers at large events along with a certificate to validate the flammable awnings that are used to cover your trade stand

- That fire-fighting equipment is readily available and is suitable for the types of fire likely to ensue
- That a quick exit can be made in the event of a fire
- That escape exits are not obstructed by tables, chairs and boxes

Your responsibilities as a face painter are to:

- Keep flammable products away from heat or ignition sources (such as skin & work surface cleansers)
- Avoid overloading electrical circuits
- Switch off and unplug electrical appliances when not in use
- Avoid trailing leads from electrical items or airbrush equipment, where they can be tripped over
- Avoid placing towels over electric or gas heaters

Should you be faced with a small fire you should tackle it with an extinguisher that has been provided or smother it with a fire blanket. Otherwise evacuate, and alert someone in authority immediately. Never risk injury to fight a fire.

Consumer Protection

It is important to be aware of consumer legislation in the unfortunate event of having to deal with a customer seeking compensation for products or services received. Therefore it is essential that you have a good understanding of what is involved in relation to the face painting service provided. A disappointed customer could take action against you if they felt that reasonable care had not been taken.

This Act covers consumer protection with regards to:

- A customer becoming injured by a defective face painting product. Ensure that the products you use are US Food & Drug Administration (FDA) or European Union Cosmetics Directive (EU) approved
- A customer becoming injured due to a negligent face painting service. Ensure that you abide to the industry code of practice, using safe methods of application
- A customer may become unwell if they came into immediate contact with a known allergen (something that causes a reaction). It's wise to remember here that many people have a nut allergy so be aware of eating a peanut butter sandwich or a Snickers bar during your lunch-break when out providing your face painting service as traces of nut oil may be present on your hands which could cause a reaction

Supply of Goods and Services

This Act gives consumer protection on the face painting service provided. A disappointed customer would need to prove that reasonable care had not been taken by the face painter prior to taking any further action.

Trades Description

It is a criminal offence to describe goods or services falsely, therefore when giving a description to a customer on the sale of goods or on the provision of a service it must be a true claim.

This Act prohibits the use of false descriptions and covers:

- Advertising, display cards and business cards. All printed material must not mislead the customer leading to the wrong information given about the face painting service which will also include using other painters photographed work which has not been done by your hand
- Verbal descriptions. You must describe your face painting service correctly and not allow the customer to believe they are getting something quite different, maybe more advanced than your skill allows
- The price you charge for your service must reflect the standard and quality of your ability, but at the same time be kept in line as close as possible to other similar service providers. Price indications reflect national expectations and quality of service
- The customer should receive what is described in the display material with regards to quantity of application, i.e., basic cheek art or full face painting

- Misleading prices on products or services. The customer will always pay the price that is displayed in your literature or on any signage displayed

Control of Substances Hazardous to Health

COSHH - This law requires control to people's exposure to hazardous substances in the work place. Some highly flammable products such as surgical spirit (used for work surface cleansing, brush cleansing and skin cleansing), isopropyl rubbing alcohol (used in tattoo applications) and methylated spirit (used in stencil cleansing) are safe in normal circumstances, but can become hazardous if exposed to a heat or an ignition source and other certain conditions.

The manufactures instructions relating to the use and storage of these products must always be followed and will generally imply that:

- Hazardous substances must be stored in a cool dry place away from direct sunlight

- Heat, ignition sources and smoking is not allowed in the vicinity of any hazardous substances

Personal Protective Equipment

If it is necessary for you to wear personal protective equipment, such as latex gloves, for whatever reason then you must obtain adequate information and instruction or training in use.

For example:

- What risks are present to the face painter and to the customer and why is the PPE needed. Latex gloves can pose an allergy reaction to some customers
- What factors could affect the performance of the face painter, in turn providing limitations to the service provided, such as the wearing of gloves

Accidents, Spillages and Waste

All accidents that occur in the work place must be reported and entered into an accident register. This is a requirement of the Health & Safety Act.

The procedure in the event of an accident is to:

- Report the accident to a person in authority, i.e. the booker
- Enter the details of the accident into the register. This would include your name, the casualties name & age,

date, place of incident, description of accident and any first aid applied

- If requested, a written report should be sent to the Health & Safety officer

The procedure for mitigating accidents, spillages and waste are as follows:

- Keep all items such as kit boxes, stock and any other equipment boxes or carriers well out of the way of the public to prevent tripping hazards
- Ensure any trailing electrical leads are taped-down onto a flat surface and that any guy-ropes attached to a gazebo or stall are clearly identified with an obvious marked indicator such as colourful bunting
- If it is a floor spill from your water cup this must be wiped up immediately and customers should be warned that the area is wet and could be slippery. Display a sign if necessary
- Clear up waste items and dispose of them immediately, such as used cleansing wipes and cotton pads. A lined container/bucket/bin should be kept under the face painting table solely for this purpose
- Should a glass item be broken it must be wrapped in paper first before placing into the refuse bin, better still it should be placed in a sharps bin

Basic First Aid

An occasion may arise when you are needed to give First Aid to minor injuries, if those holding relevant qualifications are unavailable. The following guidelines are provided based on advice from the UK Health & Safety Executive.

1. Ensure that your own cuts and abrasions are covered prior to treating a casualty
2. The wearing of surgical gloves is advisable
3. Thoroughly wash your hands before and after the treatment is given
4. If any blood or body fluids need mopping up use disposable paper and wear a disposable apron
5. Place all disposable items in a refuse sack and destroy by incineration (or hand in to the Health & Safety personnel)
6. Boil wash any contaminated clothing
7. Clean contaminated work surfaces with household bleach using a 1:10 dilution. This will destroy the AIDS virus
8. If direct contact with body fluids occur, wash hands immediately with anti-bacterial soap and water
9. Mouth to mouth resuscitation carries a risk of infection. Use an airway device for this purpose.

A First Aid kit should be readily available for use should you, an employee or a customer becomes ill or injured whilst in your work area.

Security in The Workplace

It is your responsibility to ensure that your personal belongings and those of your customers are safe for the duration of the face painting service provision. However, workplace policies can usually reflect that they will not be held responsible for loss, damage or theft of personal property.

As a minimum precaution:

- Bags should be kept in a safe area, preferably under your work station
- Purses and mobile phones should be kept out of sight
- Money and valuables bought into the work area should be kept to a minimum
- Adequate provision should be made for the safe-keeping of monies taken for services rendered

Public Liability Insurance

As you may be well aware, we live in a claims conscience society and it is a *requirement and a necessity* for you as a face painter to have adequate public liability insurance. The policy will have a condition that you exercise reasonable care in carrying out your work. It is imperative therefore that due care and diligence is demonstrated to ensure your full policy cover applies.

The level of indemnity will vary according to the face painting activities that you will be performing:

- Cover of £2million indemnity will give protection for working at children's parties in private homes and community centres, at school fetes and at small village fun days
- Cover of £5million indemnity will be needed if you intend to face paint for larger corporations such as councils, shopping centres, and at shows and festivals

If you are a beauty therapist and already hold beauty public liability insurance you should contact your provider to add face painting to your list of services, however these days there are many insurance providers that specialise in specific face painting indemnity.

Age Restriction Policies

Once you have organised your public liability insurance and have your policies in place it's important to read through the small print with regards to any age restrictions that you may have written in.

Some insurance providers stipulate that you should not paint anyone under the age of 36 months, and this is due to the fact that children under that age have sensitive skin and their immune system is still in development. They have not yet built up a tolerance to a lot of external substances and cosmetics may be too harsh for their delicate skin and could in fact lead to them having a future reaction to any ingredients that the water make-up product may have.

If your policy does not stipulate any age restriction then it will be up to you as an individual painter to make the decision for yourself as to whether you will face paint the under 3's or not. This topic has been open to great debate and all I can advise you here is that if the toddler is very happy to be painted, wants to be painted, and the parent is in agreement with this then you can use your own discretion. As a company we've painted many, many under 3's following that as a guideline and as long as the child is not wriggling around or is distressed in any way we are happy to paint 'a little something' of their face.

Another policy that you must put in place is that you shouldn't paint any child who is under the age of 16 years that has no parent/carer with them. We provide our face painting service at many funfairs and this is the usual place where young teens hang out without their Mums and Dads, and are keen to usually have some sort of eye enhancement painted on. We ask those youngsters waiting in line how old they are, and because of the nature of the service being provided they usually think that you're going to say that they're too old, so they say with a confused look we're 12. It's then we ask them if their parent is with them as we need permission to paint them as they are classed as a minor (which makes them look even more confused!). If the answer is 'no parent' then the only thing we can do is ask for a text message to come in from their Mum on their phone or to actually get her on the phone so I can ask if it's okay to paint her daughter. This can be so very difficult as it can't be policed properly as the text message displayed could be from anyone. Again another age policy that you as a face painter will need to think long and hard about and how you will enforce it.

Risk Assessments

Risk assessments are regarded as essential good practices. The foundation on completing a risk assessment is basic common sense. You need to identify potential hazards along with those who may come to harm, and then identify the necessary action to mitigate the risk. It really is that simple – identify the risk, and then work out how to prevent it from happening. A face painter's risk assessment will look for hazards which you could reasonably expect a result of slight to significant harm such as product reaction, the conditions that cause it, who might be harmed and how the risk will be controlled.

As well as identifying the usual risks such as product reaction, inadequate training, handling of waste and erecting outside structures such as gazebos – you will also need to be aware of the risks of painting children who are asleep (which goes back to your age restriction policy) and painting adults who are intoxicated, abusive and violent.

Many large corporate bookers requiring a face painting service at their event will now ask you to supply a risk assessment.

See sample Risk Assessment at the back of this book.

Method Statements

Sometimes as a face painter you will need to submit a method statement to attend some of the larger shows and festivals. This document will provide a brief description of all activities encountered from the moment you arrive at the showground to the time that you leave. The health and safety officials require specific examples relating to all areas of work and participation at their event.

Points that you will need to verify are how you will unload, move and set-up your equipment, how you will check for hazards, how the trade-stand/market-stall will be secured to the ground, how the goods/products will be displayed, how you converse with customers to make your sales and how you ensure the safety of your takings.

See sample Method Statement at the end of this book.

CRB Check Requirements

As a face painter it is not a necessity to have a CRB (criminal record bureau) check as we are not in sole care of children, however it is highly desirable to have one. Bookers will often seek a number of quotations from various face painting companies in the area, and some will ask if you have one in place. If you do have a CRB it will go a long way to securing more events for you.

CRB checks are done on your criminal history from the past so that means that unfortunately when they are issued to you they are automatically out of date! Nevertheless – they are well worth having.

It is fairly straightforward to obtain a self certified CRB check and this can be done online through www.disclosurescotland.co.uk at a minimal cost.

Internet and Photo Release Requirements

Building a portfolio of photographic evidence is paramount to the promotion of any face painting business as it is a very visual and creative industry. Your photographs will form part of your display and promotion and may also be used in your sales material and on any future website.

On the completion of painting the perfect face on a child (or adult for that matter) you will need to gain permission to take photographic evidence to use for your benefit. Images of children on the Internet are classed as personal data under the Data Protection Act 1998. Therefore using such images for publicity purposes requires the consent of the *legal* guardian (parent, adoptive parent or foster parent) and cannot be consented for by grandparents or other family members.

An Internet/Photographic Release form is what you will need to complete as standard practice. This document will detail the particulars of the person being photographed, explain what the photograph will be used for and its limitations and will bear the confirmation signature of the legal guardian responsible.

Release forms to be used should always be kept in your kit as you never know when you are going to need one.

See sample Internet Release Form at the back of this book.

Code of Practice

We've just covered some important subject matters relating to good working practices within our face painting industry, and below is a code of practice that summarises many of those values above.

1. Take reasonable care to avoid injury to you and to others paying particular attention to accidents, spillages and waste. You must not interfere or misuse anything provided to protect you and your customer's safety.

2. Hold a current certificate for public liability protection. Your indemnity should be between £2-£5 million.

3. Ensure that all products and equipment used are safe the intended purpose which will prevent a customer from becoming injured by defective merchandise or an inferior face painting application.

4. Be conversant with product ingredients, familiar with administrating patch tests and dealing with customer allergy declaration forms as and when they arise.

5. Conform to any age restrictions that are in place by insurance providers and only proceed if the customer is suitable and appropriate in all measures for the face painting application.

6. To reflect the professionalism of the industry, your appearance should be clean and neat. Tie back long hair, keep jewellery to a minimum and nails should ideally be short. Keep your work area sanitary, tidy and organised during the session.

7. Do not paint anyone's face if a contra-indication is present or suspected and patch test anyone with a known allergy. Cover any cuts or abrasions of your own with a waterproof dressing. Always display a Health & Safety disclaimer notice at all events.

8. Cleanse faces with a facial cleansing/baby wipe prior to makeup application and dispose of all waste wipes immediately in a lined bin. Change your brush water frequently and wipe over brushes intermittently with a surgical spirit solution.

9. Customers should be advised on the basic steps of removal, i.e., wash the area with warm soapy water, rinse and apply a moisturiser or use cleansing wipes.

10. Face paints and palettes should be cleaned after each session with surgical spirit, brushes and water cups washed and then sterilised in a solution, and sponges should be washed in a washing machine and left to air-dry.

CHAPTER 13

So Where To Now?

Adding Additional Services

Once you have been bitten by the face painting bug and your business is ticking along nicely with a steady stream of events you may find yourself looking to expand your service provision on what you can next offer to your ready and waiting audience.

One of the easiest additional services to add to your repertoire is the very popular Glitter Tattoo. In the late 1990's we could see the potential in these so we added this service and in those early days the tattoos were applied by hand with coloured liquid latex and glitter. Applying the glitter tattoos in a free-hand method did mean that an element of artistic skill was needed in order to paint on such intricate designs using the latex. Luckily these days glitter tattoos are so easy to apply with the use of a pre-cut self-adhesive stencil that is just peeled away from its backing strip, which is then applied to the sanitised skin and painted over with skin glue and then loose glitter is pressed into the glue. The stencil is then peeled away to display a fantastic glitter creation. What could be easier?

Another fantastic service line to add on is Henna Bodyart. This does need a certain amount of practice as it's best to apply this type of art free-hand and you'll need to build up your skill just like face painting, and as henna is easily available as a pre-blended mix it's worth purchasing a cone to have a go at.

Over the years Mimicks has introduced a variety of service lines to add on and compliment with our face painting, and there's no reason why you too shouldn't think outside of the paint pot and start expanding your business portfolio:

1990:
Mimicks started with just a face painting service
1992:
Next came a range of temporary tattoos by Wild at Heart
1993:
We started hair braid wraps and plaits and hair colouring
1994:
Horribly realistic fake wounds were a massive hit
1998:
Next came the introduction of the popular henna bodyart
2000:
Trendy coloured hair extensions came along in this year
2002:
Saw the launch of the free-hand glitter tattoos
2003:
Then we started applying airbrushed body art

2004:

Princess pamper parties were started and a new company – Once Upon A Party - was formed (and then sold in 2010)

2009:

We introduced corporate body painting

2011:

Baby bump painting to expectant mums was next

2012:

Eye enhancements for hen parties came next

So as you can see it was a gradual process in building the company that we are today. Some of the service lines have come and gone and some have stayed with us over time, and being in a very creative make-up industry we're always on the lookout for the next hot trend.

Developing Your Creative Skill

Remember those good old school days, and especially those art classes - don't you wish you'd paid just a little bit more attention to colour theory and values, shading and highlighting along with composition and perspective!

It's never too late to go back to college and enrol on one of the many different types of adult education art courses that are now available to you. There you will learn and get a better understanding of art in its entirety from basic skills through to the more advanced techniques. This will be time and money well spent as you'll gain practical knowledge in a wealth of useful tips and techniques that you can then transfer straight into your face painting business.

The same principle applies to learning the art of photography as this will enhance your photographic evidence that you'll be able to use on your company website and other sales material. Capturing your face painted creations as and when they happen with the correct camera settings, the best angle and the most excellent lighting possibilities will certainly enhance your work.

For more information on art courses and photographic courses just check out the adult education pages on the websites of your local colleges.

If you have the opportunity to enrol on either an art course or a photographic course then do so, but my strong recommendation to you would be to sign-up for a beauty related course as it's the best investment in yourself that you can make.

There are many beauty courses held at local colleges and adult education centres that run a diverse range of awards, certificates and diplomas that you can train in. You don't necessarily need to go back to college full-time as a lot of them are run on a part-time basis which usually means over one evening per week.

Look out for courses such as Cosmetic Make-up, Fashion & Photographic Make-up and Make-up Artistry (which includes the Face and Body Art unit) which will provide you with a wealth of underpinning knowledge and some very useful creative make-up skills that will be assignable to your face painting business or for you to offer as an additional service to your customers. If you're in a position to return to college on a full-time basis (which is usually 16-18 hours per week) then I would recommended the Theatrical, Special Effects and Media Make-up course. Oh and of course, don't rule out any of the Creative Hair Styling courses as well. If you don't quite fancy the college environment then there are a number of private training establishments that also offer accredited qualifications and those that run certificated short-courses in a diverse range of beauty, hair and make-up applications.

If you purely want to progress in just your face painting skills and you want to train over just a couple of days then there are many instructors out there to choose from. Some trainers may in fact be local to you and there are those who travel the World with their touring classes at a selection of locations. Check out your training provider first to check for longevity in the industry, that they can offer a broad and diverse range of techniques and that their work is to the benchmark that you'd like to replicate.

It's now time for you to:
Start Your Successful Face Painting Business

As a quick re-cap think back to what's been covered here in this book. We've discussed:

- ✓ What it takes to be your own boss –
  You now understand what a fulfilling, exciting and sometimes scary experience it can be being self-employed as it will all be solely down to you on how you discipline yourself in order to grow your business into a successful and financially rewarding one

- ✓ Working from home and dealing with distractions –
  You now recognise that in order to achieve business growth through promotion you must deal with the daily distractions that you will encounter in an effective manner so that you can actually put in the un-disturbed man-hours to work *on* your business rather than just *in* your business

- ✓ Building your brand -
  You'll understand how choosing a business name which will become a major part of your branding is of significant importance on how you will influence your customer and their expectations

- ✓ Putting yourself out there -
  You'll be able to confidently become proactive with regards to self promotion and how to capture your

very first bank of customers which is essential for the early stages of business start-up

✓ Face painting at events -
You will be able to identify with the huge opportunities that are waiting out there for you at a variety of events that you can offer your face painting service to

✓ Your workplace set-up –
You'll now have the self-assurance to make a good lasting impression with a well-organized work area and be able to maintain a professional attitude with regards to all of the event protocol expectations

✓ Customer care and communication –
You'll be more aware of how to effectively interact through conversation with your customers and also how to proficiently work on and care for them regardless as to whether they are children or adults

✓ Putting systems in place -
You'll now be able to plan for a comprehensive and consistently branded business administration system that will take care of all the necessary documents that you'll need in the early stages of your venture

✓ Products and equipment -
You'll have a better understanding of the diverse range of products, tools and equipment that are

available to you to add to your ever-expanding face painting kit

✓ Maintaining industry standards -
You'll be aware of current legislation, industry standards and safe working practices that you'll need to follow in order to comply with the law which will help you to promote a safe working environment

Oh and don't forget, if this book has encouraged you to go full steam ahead now that you've been bitten by the face painting bug and are eager to learn more business fundamentals for growth, then my follow-on book will be a great inspiration for you as it covers in great detail the following topics:

Growing Your Highly Profitable
Face Painting Business

✓ Organisation and Action Planning
Plan out your goals to get you going in order to achieve the life you really want by taking consistent action in key business areas

✓ Your Target Market
Understand just who your customer is and become perceptive to their needs by developing a service provision that is exclusively for them

✓ What Does Your Customer Want?
Get the most out of your customers by building on the know, like, trust factor and really discover what problem of theirs you can solve

✓ Developing Relationships
How to build, grow and nurture your customer list by developing an ongoing relationship campaign with them to boost your sales

✓ Adding Value
Learn how to stop selling and how to start giving to your customers instead by fulfilling their needs, wants and desires by adding immense value to their lives

✓ Setting Your Prices
How you can set your service rates for maximum profit by analyzing your current income streams, knowing then that you are being paid what you so rightly deserve

✓ Business Planning
Writing objective, cash flow and financial business plans so you know where you're going and how you're going to get there

✓ Legal Requirements
Keeping on the right side of the law with a dependable accounting system and knowing how to

organise your comprehensive book-keeping paperwork in order to stay on top of it all

✓ Marketing Plan
How to focus on a well structured marketing plan so you know what results you are achieving every step of the way with regards to your content, headlines and call to actions

✓ Advertising Online and Offline
Discover a diverse array of marketing strategies that are available for you to advertise and promote your face painting business without it breaking the bank

✓ Your Sales Process
How to make a huge difference with an effective sales process. If you were the customer would buying your service be the right choice or is there a better option available on the market. What are you doing that your competitor isn't?

✓ Testimonial Collection
No-one says it better than your customer, so know how to make better use of your testimonials and how to integrate them into all your advertising as standard practice to build your influential social proof

✓ Golden Opportunities
Looking out for and spotting those all important lucky breaks that are generally presented to you more often than not

✓ Keeping Customers Informed
Keep your existing customers up to date with exciting new services and products and how to add on cross-selling and up-selling as an incentive for them to buy from you

Face Painting For Profit - Mimicks
An innovative marketing advice club for the Face Painting industry's business owners – like you

Stuck for marketing ideas, want to get an inside look on how the experts of the industry are doing it or need to ramp up your social media marketing strategies? Then at Face Painting For Profit you will find all the inspiration you could possibly need to help grow you business to its next level. FPFP is a membership club for small business owners just like you where your challenges and reservations are answered by people who have been there, done that. There are plenty of free articles at the club in a variety of topics for you to browse through or you can become a fully-fledged club member and have elite access to additional marketing resources. See you over there. **www.facepaintingforprofit.co.uk**

Face Painting Academy - Mimicks
New to Face Painting? – Then The Academy is for you

Sometimes being a new face painter in the industry can be quite a daunting prospect in knowing how to get those first birthday parties and company events. The Face Painting Academy is a place where you can be listed as a 'New' face painter looking for work without having the worry factor of skill, speed and longevity in the industry. With every booking that you secure through the Academy will be one step closer in adding to your expertise as a first-class face painter. And better still – a fantastic way for you to promote yourself and your new business to the masses.

www.facepaintingacademy.com

I wish you all the very best in your new business venture and would very much like to hear how you're getting along. Your success as a new face painter in our industry means a lot to me and if you have any stories to tell, questions to be answered or any face painting issues that you'd like to discuss you can contact me anytime at sherrill@mimicks.co.uk

Well that's it. You should now find yourself armed with all the essential knowledge, know-how and practical advice that you'll need in

Starting Your Super Successful
Face Painting Business

Sherrill Church

Sample Documents

Sample Documents

Over the next few pages I have included some simple sample documents for you to copy and use in your business administration. There are of course many other types of documents that you will need in order to set up your complete business system, but for starters I've shown the ones that will be most important in getting you going.

If you would like a FREE copy of any of the documents sent straight to you by email so that you can tweak and edit them to your heart's content then please email me and I'll send the Word.docx over to you.

sherrill@mimicks.co.uk

COMPANY INVOICE

Your Logo and Address

Invoice To	# 1398
	Date invoice sent
Customers Name	
Customers Address	**INVOICE**

Event Details	Terms	Reference
[details of the type of event]	14 [21,30] days	Their reference

Date	Time	Service Details	Total
12.12.12	1.00pm – 4.00pm	Face Painting	£------

Total Payable	£------
Deposit Paid [date]	£------
Balance Due	£------

Cheque payable to [your business name]

BACS Payments: [your bank account details]

Thank you for your custom and we look forward to being of service to you again

CONFIRMATION OF BOOKING
FOR BIRTHDAY PARTIES

Your Logo and Address

CONFIRMATION OF PARTY BOOKING

CUSTOMER NAME	Jenifer Brown
ADDRESS	123 The Avenue Sometown Someplace Postcode
VENUE ADDRESS	Village Community Centre Sometown Postcode
TELEPHONE NUMBERS	023 123 456 / 07777 888999
EMAIL ADDRESS	jenifer@mail.co.uk
SERVICE DETAILS	Face Painting
TYPE OF EVENT	Katie's 7th Birthday Party
EVENT DATE	Saturday 12th January
TIME	3.00pm – 5.00pm
ARTISTE	Sherrill
COST	£------

£40 deposit to be paid by return.
Cheque made payable to [business name]
Bank Transfer to [bank account details]

TERMS AND CONDITIONS
FOR PARTIES AND PRIVATE EVENTS

Terms and Conditions: **Parties and Private Events**

1. On booking your party with [company name] they will send you a confirmation outlining the details of your event.
2. To confirm your booking, a £40 non-returnable deposit cheque must be forwarded to the company address within 7 days. Should this payment not be made then they reserve the right to cancel the booking.
3. The artiste(s) will arrive 5-10 minutes prior to their start time in order to set-up their products and equipment.
4. Parking fees, if applicable, will be reflected in your price. Please inform [company name] at the time of booking if this is the case. For permit located areas, please arrange for a car parking space for the artiste.
5. Please arrange for a suitable cover/shade/gazebo should our artiste(s) be working outside.
6. The artiste(s) will work with no stoppages until all the willing guests have been worked on. Please do not include a birthday tea break during their performance as the artiste(s) will need to work on a continuous basis. If the birthday tea needs to take place during their stay they will carry on with as little disruption as possible.
7. If more guests than previously anticipated wish to be worked on it will be left to the discretion of the artiste(s) as to whether they can be accommodated or not, depending on other commitments.
8. [Company name] artiste(s) will not work on anyone with a skin disease or disorder, or anyone who is threatening to their safety or anyone who is under the influence of alcohol and will have a health and safety disclaimer clearly displayed relating to the effect.
9. After packing away their products they will be unable to re-set up again should a late-comer arrive to the party.
10. [Company name] are not held responsible in the event on non-fulfilment of the engagement by our artiste(s), however every reasonable safeguard is assured. Deposits will be refunded in full.
11. Cancellation of the party by the customer must be given in writing no fewer than 7 days prior to the performance in order to prevent being charged a 75% non-fulfilment fee.
12. Cancellations made on the day of the party will be liable for payment in full.
13. [Company name] maintain a high standard of work with professional products and follow the industry's code of practice.

CONFIRMATION OF BOOKING
FOR CORPORATE BOOKERS

Your Logo and Address

CONFIRMATION OF CORPORATE BOOKING

CONTACT NAME	Dave Smith
COMPANY	The Toy Shop
INVOICE ADDRESS	123 The High Street Sometown Someplace Postcode
VENUE ADDRESS	As above Sometown Postcode
COMPANY TELEPHONE NUMBER	023 456 789
EVENT CONTACT DETAILS	Sally 07777 123456
EMAIL ADDRESS	shop@mail.co.uk
SERVICE DETAILS	Face Painting
TYPE OF EVENT	Shop Launch
EVENT DATE	Saturday 12th January
TIME	11.00pm – 4.00pm
ARTISTE(s)	Sherrill and Ashlea
COST	£------

TERMS AND CONDITIONS
FOR CORPORATE BOOKERS

Terms and Conditions: **Corporate Events**

1. Submission of a booking and its acceptance by [company name] shall constitute a contract between the company and the booker and will not be deemed as confirmed until [company name] has received your signed confirmation.
2. The invoice will be raised by [company name] immediately after the event on a strict 14 {21, 30} day payment term. Additional percentage fees will be added for late payments.
3. For pay on the day arrangements, cheque's are made payable to [company name]
4. [Company name] are not held responsible in the event of non-fulfilment of the engagement by our artiste(s), however every reasonable safeguard is assured.
5. Cancellation of the event by you the booker must be given in writing no fewer than 14 days prior to the event. Cancellations made between 14-21 days prior will be subject to a 25% administration charge, 1-13 days a 50% charge and on the day cancellations will be liable for payment in full due to loss of booking.
6. The artiste(s) will arrive approximately 15-20 minutes prior to their start time. Should you require them in place prior to their start time then this will be reflected in the price.
7. Parking fees to attend your event will be reflected in your price. Please inform us at the time of booking should this be the case.
8. [Company name] artiste(s) arrive fully equipped with products and equipment, however the provision of an outside shelter is required by you, should your event be outside to protect against the elements.
9. Each artiste will take a 10 minute break for every 90 minutes worked - after an initial two-hours.
10. The artiste(s) will not work on anyone with a skin disease or disorder, or anyone who is threatening to their safety or anyone who is under the influence of alcohol and will have a health and safety disclaimer clearly displayed relating to the effect.
11. After packing away their products and equipment they will be unable to re-set up again should late-comers arrive to your event.
12. [Company name] maintain a high standard of work with professional products and follow the industry's code of practice.

RISK ASSESSMENT

Face Painting **Risk Assessment**

Who can be Affected			
A	**B**	**C**	**D**
You or Staff	Public	Contractors	Buildings

Likelihood of Risk Happening					
1	**2**	**3**	**4**	**5**	**6**
Very Unlikely	Unlikely to happen	May Occur	Likely to happen	Very Likely to happen	Will Occur

Severity of Injury					
1	**2**	**3**	**4**	**5**	**6**
No Injury	Slight Injury	Mild Injury	Minor Injury	Major Injury	Fatality

Risk Factor		
A	**B**	**C**
Low Factor 0-10 Little or no action required	**Medium Factor 11-20** Some action possible with review as required	**High Factor 21-30** Immediate action and further controls required

	Description of Hazard / Risk	Affected A-D	Likelihood 1-6	Severity 1-6	Risk 1-30
1					
2					
3					

	Control Measures to be taken for above Hazards / Risks:
1	
2	
3	

Assessed by: Signed: Dated:

....

GENERAL HAZARDS AND RISKS

Face Painting Hazards and Risks

Hazard / Risk	Control Measures
Vehicle movement	Service vehicle driving around site, not exceeding 5mph taking due care of persons within the immediate vicinity and other stalls and equipment.
Temporary Structure Stall or Gazebo	All 4 corners tied down with ratchets and pegs on grassed areas and weights and straps on hard-standing areas to secure stall/gazebo to ground to prevent tipping over in excessive strong winds.
Manual handling	Stock boxes having no more than 3kg in weight. Correct posture when lifting boxes.
Working at heights	Setting up and breaking down of stall/gazebo to be erected using a stable and safe stepladder.
Spillages and Waste	All spillages to be mopped up immediately and area made safe, and all refuse placed into receptacle and to be removed to site waste container when necessary.
Staff Welfare	All team members to be fully aware of risks and how to control them and to be adequately informed or trained in product and equipment use where relevant.
Service Products and Equipment	Only FDA/EU approved products used, which complies with the recognised industry standard along with its code of practice. All products and equipment must be suitable for their purpose and intended use.

ALLERGY DECLARATION FORM

Face Painting Allergy Declaration

[Company Information goes here]

Please read, sign and date the allergy declaration below.

I understand that I take full risk and hold all responsibility for the face painting application to be administered to my child by [company] even though I am aware that he/she has a known intolerance/allergy to face painting products and has had a reaction in the past.

My child has had a 30-minute patch test administered on her wrist and the company [company name] has advised me that a reaction may still take place as this is by no measure a guarantee for a negative patch test result.

I grant permission for the face painting application to proceed on my child and I take full responsibility for the risk involved:

.... *(insert child's name)*

I am the legal guardian of the above named child.

Print Name ....

Signed...

Dated ....

INTERNET AND PHOTOGRAPHIC
RELEASE FORM

Face Painting

Internet and Photographic Release Policy

[Company Information goes here]

Images of children on the Internet are classed as personal data under the Data Protection Act 1998. Therefore using such images for publicity purposes requires the consent of the legal guardian.

Please read, sign and date the declaration below.

I understand that the photographic images used of my child on the [company name] website, and any of their promotional material (i.e., leaflets, brochures, and business cards) will be used solely for marketing purposes. I acknowledge that [company name] will not be held responsible in the event that the image is down-loaded from their website by a third party and used for other purposes.

I grant permission for the photographic images of my child to be used:

.. (insert child's name)

I am the legal guardian of the above named child.

Print Name ....

Signed...

Dated ....

METHOD STATEMENT

Face Painting Method Statement

1. Arrive at event and check in at site office to be shown trade space allocated.
2. Drive slowly, with hazard lights on, to the allocated trade space keeping within a 5mph speed limit.
3. Check your allocated trade space for any hazards.
4. Unload stall/gazebo taking due precaution and care.
5. Erect stall/gazebo following the manufacturer's guidelines and secure at each corner with ratchets and pegs into grassed areas or weights and straps on a hard-standing areas.
6. Unload equipment from the vehicle and set up ensuring that tables and chairs are safe for their intended use and walkways are kept clear with no obstructions.
7. Unload products and set-out in a safe and efficient working order.
8. Park vehicle in allocated site either next to trade stand or in trader's car park. Display company details inside vehicle on windscreen.
9. Display price signs for services rendered with clear and accurate information.
10. During the event speak to customers and make and provide service sales.
11. Ensure appropriate monies are collected giving out the correct change where necessary and that takings are stored safely.
12. Remove waste materials to the appropriate bin provided.
13. At end of day pack away all products and equipment and dissemble the stall/gazebo.
14. Bring vehicle back onto show ground, driving slowly with hazard lights on.
15. Pack products, equipment and stall/gazebo back into vehicle.
16. Provide a final check to the trade space area to ensure no hazards are left behind.
17. Leave showground, driving slowly with hazard lights on.

Resources

Product Suppliers

Mimicks Face Painting

➤ Whether you're a seasoned professional face painter in the industry or have recently started and been bitten by the face painting bug, or even just had your very first inclination to get going in a new and exciting venture - then we have all the face painting products that your heart could possibly desire. The Mimicks team have been face painting for over two decades and have been supplying products to the trade for just as long. With an abundance of products available on the market today, the items sold on their website have all be used extensively by Sherrill and Ashlea and a lot are endorsed on the MimicksTV Youtube channel where you can see the products being used to their full glory.

www.facepainting.uk.com

Facade

➤ Your online shop for quality YBODY Glitter and Airbrush Tattoo products, along with the best range of stencils and cosmetic glitters available in the UK. Our stencils, glues and glitters are the preferred choice of professional face and body artists around the world. Try them and you will soon realise why! We also offer a full range of Iwata Compressors, Airbrushes and Body Art products. We are the UK distributor for Cameleon face and body paint.

www.facadebodyart.co.uk

The Face Painting Shop

➤ The Face Painting Shop was set up by professional face painters who have been in the business for over 15 years, working with many celebrities and blue chip companies. We know the best products to stock and are always on hand to help with advice and tips. We are your one-stop shop that stocks the full ranges of Superstar, Snazaroo, Diamond FX, Silly Farm, ShowOff body art stencils and Charles Fox.

www.thefacepaintingshop.com

SillyFarm

> ➤ SillyFarm is the largest specialized store for everything face and body art, catering to the needs of all sorts of artists. Whether you are a novice face painter or an experienced body painter Silly Farm has what you want and need. With a team of twenty seven employees, that are talented painters in their own right, they are eager and willing to help you reach your face and body art goals. Each staff member has extensive product knowledge and can guide you through the 5,000 products we carry.

www.sillyfarm.com

Dauphines

> ➤ We are a supplier of top-quality makeup and wigs and have been in the theatrical business for a generation providing theatres, operatic societies, drama groups, face painters and the public alike. Our ranges include water-based makeup, cream makeup, camouflage make-up, brushes and glitter... you name it, we supply it, Nationally and Internationally as well.

www.dauphines.co.uk

Training Providers

Mimicks Face Painting

> ➤ Mimicks Courses in Face Painting, Henna Body Art, Glitter Tattoos and Casualty Make-up have the potential to be of great value should you be seeking a new hobby or interest, as well as increasing your income stream. Each course explores what it will take for you to apply creative make-up techniques and the importance of using the correct products and equipment to improve your skills. Consisting of fully comprehensive, practical and rewarding sessions will provide you with the expert advice necessary to get you started.

www.facepaintingtraining.com

Facade

➢ The Facade Academy of Face and Body Art is located in a superb modern facility at the Paradise Wildlife Park in Hertfordshire. Our courses include Face painting for all levels and specialties, Body Painting, Introductory Course in Airbrushing and we have occasional courses by guest instructors who are at the top of their game. www.facadebodyart.co.uk

Treasure House – The Make-up Academy

➢ Our focus is to provide makeup artists and students with the necessary skills for their professional advancement within the Cosmetics Industries. We offer a vocational experience guaranteed to satisfy and enhance the training of the most eager and demanding students. All of our courses have been developed with the support and knowledge of industry leaders that incorporate the most up-to-date techniques and products. We provide courses in Body Painting, Airbrushing, Casualty and Special Effects, Fashion and Beauty, TV and Film. Visit our website today for more information. www.treasurehouseofmakeup.co.uk

Capital Hair and Beauty

➢ We are a hair and beauty wholesaler who offer a wide range of accredited make-up, beauty and hair courses using both local independent specialists and national training companies. Our aim is to give you affordable and professional hair and beauty training in your area combined with an enjoyable and fun day that will give you another skill or technique to add to your menu. www.capitalhairandbeauty.co.uk

Tutorial Contributors

Ashlea Henson – Mimicks Face Painting

> ➤ Ashlea is the creative partner at Mimicks Face Painting and has been producing tutorial videos for a number of years. If you're new to face painting Ashlea will inspire you with just how far you can go in this wonderful creative industry. She enjoys passing on her face painting skills and has a good selection of tutorials aimed at beginners through to the more advanced artistes. Check Ashlea out at: www.Youtube.com/MimicksTV

FabaTV

> ➤ Taking online face and body art classes from the world's best instructors has never been easier. You no longer have to take days off of work, travel, find a sitter, or re-arrange your schedule to be able to take face and body art classes. We offer quality training on your time, at your pace, in the comfort of your own home! What more can you ask for? At FABAtv.com can you find classes covering every aspect of face and body art including classes on face painting, airbrushing, Black light body art, marketing, henna, and so much more. Visit them at: www.fabatv.com

Magazines and Directories

Illusion Magazine

> ➤ Without a doubt, this is the best printed publication to hit the face and body painting industry. With four editions each year, the magazine is bursting with amazing talent from across the globe. Packed full of original step-by-step artwork, artist features, industry news and reviews, this magazine is for anyone who is interested in face and body art, whether it's their hobby or passion. Illusion's online shop is also a resource in its own right and stocks face and body

painting books, DVDs, brushes, kitbags and stencils. Illusion is guaranteed to inspire you.

www.illusionmagazine.co.uk

The Showman's Directory

➢ Our directory is the definitive guide to outdoor events and services. The Showman's Directory was first published in 1968 and over the years has grown into the most comprehensive publication of its kind on the market today listing a calendar of UK outdoor events and contact details of the event organisers, Order one today! Once you've got it you'll wonder how you ever survived without it.

www.showmans-directory.co.uk

Make-up Artist Magazine

➢ Make-Up Artist magazine is read in nearly 70 countries around the world and was created in 1996 by Emmy Award-winning make-up artist Michael Key. The magazine features articles on the entertainment industry's top make-up artists, the most innovative make-up techniques, current product news and invaluable information available nowhere else. The art of make-up branches in many directions and this magazine covers them all so creatively.

www.makeupmag.com

Progressive Party

➢ The definitive source of information for all those in the party business. Progressive Party works closely with both party trade associations and trade show organisers to help create as much new business as possible in the party industry. By sharing knowledge and contacts we offer our clients more opportunities than just advertising! Product areas covered include balloons, costumes, partyware, wedding and celebration, masks, party props and scene setting, novelty products and everything in between - no matter how weird and wonderful it may be!

www.progressiveparty.co.uk

Party Party Magazine

➢ Party Party is essential reading for anyone in the party industry. Containing high interest editorial and a discerning readership provides the ideal environment for advertisers to promote their products with confidence.

www.partypartymag.co.uk

Membership and Academy Sites

Face Painting For Profit

➢ Stuck for marketing ideas, want to get an inside look on how the experts of the industry are doing it or need to ramp up your social media marketing strategies? Then at Face Painting For Profit you will find all the inspiration you could possibly need to help grow you business to its next level. FPFP is a membership club for small business owners just like you where your challenges and reservations are answered by people who have been there, done that. There are plenty of free articles at the club in a variety of topics for you to browse through or you can become a fully-fledged club member and have elite access to additional marketing resources. See you over there.

www.facepaintingforprofit.co.uk

Face Painting Academy

➢ Sometimes being a new face painter in the industry can be quite a daunting prospect in knowing how to get those first birthday parties and company events. The Face Painting Academy is a place where you can be listed as a 'New' face painter looking for work without having the worry factor of skill, speed and longevity in the industry. With every booking that you secure through the Academy will be one step closer in adding to your expertise as a first-class face painter. And better still – a fantastic way for you to promote yourself and your new business to the masses.

www.facepaintingacademy.com

Conventions and Forums

International Face and Body Art Convention

➢ The Face and Body Art International Convention -"FABAIC", is recognized as the original and premier event for the Face and Body Art community. The five-day event in Florida has all the following exciting features that you have come to know and love including cutting edge training, classes for every level and a retail marketplace. FABAIC has it all! There is no better place to learn new skills, increase your network, meet new friends and have the time of your life. www.fabiac.com

Paintopia

➢ The Paintopia Face Painting and Body Art Festival consists of workshops, competitions, trade stands and demonstrations for Face painters and Body Artists of all calibre. Our retail marquee will host all your favourite paints, glitters and books. The event opens to the general public as well on the Festival Sunday. Held at Dunston Hall in Norfolk, this is one festival not to be missed. www.paintopia.co.uk

FACE Conference

➢ Each year we hold our Annual Conference in the UK for our FACE members. This provides a great chance for lots of networking with like-minded individuals. www.facepaint.co.uk

Forums

➢ Forums for face painters. www.facepaintingchat.co.uk www.facepaintforum.com

Awarding Bodies

VTCT

➤ VTCT is the specialist awarding organisation for the hairdressing and beauty sector and the first non-unitary awarding body accredited to offer the Principal Learning for the new Diploma in Hair and Beauty Studies. Our full qualification package also covers complementary therapies, sport and active leisure, business skills and hospitality and catering.
www.vtct.org.uk

City & Guilds

➤ City & Guilds is a world leading vocational education organisation. We develop vocational qualifications across a variety of sectors that meet the needs of today's workplace, and help individuals develop their talents and abilities for future career progression. Our qualifications are delivered in more than 10,000 training centres across the world and are widely recognised and respected by employers.
www.cityandguilds.com

Insurance and Associations

Rees Astley

➤ Bespoke cover for the Entertainment Industry. Our Face Painting insurance can cover you for all things that probably will not happen, but might! Our primary focus is on providing cost effective insurance solutions for the self employed operating within defined markets. It's your ideal choice providing peace of mind by giving protection against many of the risks likely to be faced, as well as the flexibility to choose the level and extent of cover to meet individual requirements.
www.insurance4performingarts.co.uk

Blackfriars Insurance Brokers

➤ We offer highly competitive insurance for face painters with full quotations containing all premium information to help you make an informed choice. It is vital for all businesses to carry an appropriate level of liability insurance protection to enable them to defend and meet the costs of claims that maybe made against them whether this is from third parties or employees, clients and members of the public. Our specialist liability insurance team are on hand to assist you with your face painter's liability insurance.

www.blackfriarsgroup.com

FHT – Federation of Holistic Therapies

➤ Professional insurance can be confusing but all practising therapists should have it – that's why the FHT is here to help! As the leading professional association for therapists, and an authorised and regulated insurance intermediary, we really can advise you on the best type Insurance is only available to members of the association.

www.fht.org.uk

FACE – The Face Painting Association

➤ The Face Painting Association is for like minded people to get together and share ideas and problems in order to improve standards and raise the profile of face painting. FACE membership covers the whole of the world and its aims are to meet the needs of its members with the magazine, website and membership directory as well as opportunities to work together. FACE members routinely share their ideas, designs and tips with each other, this allows us to form friendships and be inspired by each other's designs and working methods.

www.facepaint.co.uk

Disclosure Scotland

➢ Should you be required to supply a basic, standard or enhanced disclosure (CRB check) then a self-certified one is available from this organisation. A Disclosure is a document containing impartial and confidential criminal history information held by the police and government departments which can be used by employers to make safer recruitment decisions. Anyone can apply for a basic disclosure in their own name.

www.disclosurescotland.co.uk

Data Protection - ICO

➢ From data protection and electronic communications to freedom of information and environmental regulations, the ICO is the UK's independent public body set up to uphold information rights in the public interest, promoting openness by public bodies and data privacy for individuals. Find out more about our responsibilities and obligations under the legislation we cover here at the Information Commissioners Office.

www.ico.org.uk

The Inland Revenue - HMRC

➢ We are the UK's tax authority. We are responsible for making sure that the money is available to fund the UK's public services and for helping families and individuals with targeted financial support. HMRC's work to make it easy for customers to deal with their taxes and get things right, by making our products and processes more simple and straightforward, and by improving our customer service.

www.hmrc.gov.uk

ABOUT THE AUTHOR

Sherrill Church is the founder of Mimicks Face Painting, which was established in 1990. Most of Sherrill's friends, family and acquaintances were keen to point out to her in those early years that 'face painting was just a fad, give it three years and it'll be over, here today gone tomorrow', and the most insulting comments heard were 'you should get a proper job, you'll never earn any money just face painting'. Well over two decades later business is still booming and Sherrill is now painting 2nd generation customers and she enjoys a satisfying and very financially rewarding lifestyle that can only come from running a successful business that she is still passionately in love with.

Sherrill's year-round working weekends consist of providing creative make-up services such as face painting, glitter tattoos and henna body art at birthday parties, school fetes, community fun-days, and shows and festivals, and is very much in demand at company events for business promotion. Her daughter Ashlea Henson, who was a young child when she started the company, is now a partner in the business and is responsible for the creative side of the company.

During the week Sherrill trains private individuals who are looking to start a face painting company and are in need of learning the basic skills to get them going in this very lucrative and fulfilling business venture. She is also a training provider for one of the large Hair and Beauty Wholesalers and her courses take her across the whole of the UK. Recently she has been providing continued professional development courses for lecturers in colleges teaching them too on how to deliver the Themed Face Painting unit by City & Guilds and VTCT in their own colleges.

People often ask her about the accomplishment and longevity of Mimicks Face Painting and how come it's been so successful over the years. It really is quite simple she says – She just has full-on passion and a strong belief in what she does, loving every moment of this five-minute wonder!

Neither the author or publisher will accept responsibility for any damages or loss that may result from using the ideas, advice or any other information that has been outlined in this book. The outcomes may not be suitable for every situation nor for every person.

The author and publisher make no warranties with respect to accuracy nor suitability of the contents of the work herein and specifically disclaim all warranties of fitness for any particular purpose.

This book is sold on the understanding that neither the author or publisher has rendered full legal advice, accounting advice or service advice as the reader should seek further professional advice where applicable.

Made in the USA
Charleston, SC
22 April 2016